South America

BY
MYRL SHIREMAN

COPYRIGHT © 1998 Mark Twain Media, Inc.

ISBN 1-58037-068-3

Printing No. CD–1301

Mark Twain Media, Inc., Publishers
Distributed by Carson-Dellosa Publishing Company, Inc.

The purchase of this book entitles the buyer to reproduce the student pages for classroom use only. Other permissions may be obtained by writing Mark Twain Media, Inc., Publishers.

All rights reserved. Printed in the United States of America.

Table of Contents

Introduction iv
Learning About Climates in South America 1
    Learning About the Tropics 2
    Learning About the Seasons 4
    Daylight and Darkness in the Tropics 6
    Temperature in the Tropics 7
    Climates in South America 10
    The Effects of Currents and Winds on Climate 12
    Learning About El Niño 14
        Reviewing What I Have Learned 15
A Historical Look at the South American Population 16
    European 16
        Spanish Conquistadors 17
        Portuguese 17
    Indians of South America 18
        Incas 18
            Reviewing What I Have Learned 21
            Discussion Questions 22
        Indians of the Amazon 23
        Araucanian Indians 23
            Reviewing What I Have Learned 24
South America Under Spain's Rule 25
    Spanish Rule Map Exercise 25
South America Gains Independence 26
    Spanish Rule and Independence Crossword Puzzle 27
Animals of South America 28
    Reviewing What I Have Learned 29
    Locating and Identifying South American Animals 30
Holidays and Festivals 31
    Reviewing What I Have Learned 32
Countries of South America Today 33
    Argentina 33
        Argentina Map Exercise 33
        Reviewing What I Have Learned 34
    Brazil 35
        Brazil Map Exercise 36
        Reviewing What I Have Learned 37
    Venezuela 38
        Venezuela Map Exercise 39
        Reviewing What I Have Learned 39
    Colombia 40
        Colombia Map Exercise 40
        Reviewing What I Have Learned 41

Peru, Ecuador, and Bolivia	42
Peru, Ecuador, and Bolivia Map Exercise	42
Ecuador	43
Ecuador Map Exercise	43
Peru	44
Peru Map Exercise	44
Bolivia	46
Bolivia Map Exercise	47
Reviewing What I Have Learned	48
Chile	49
Chile Map Exercise	50
Reviewing What I Have Learned	51
Paraguay	52
Paraguay Map Exercise	53
Reviewing What I Have Learned	54
Paraguay Crossword Puzzle	55
Uruguay	56
Uruguay Map Exercise	56
Reviewing What I Have Learned	57
Surinam, Guyana, and French Guiana	58
Surinam, Guyana, and French Guiana Map Exercise	59
Reviewing What I Have Learned	60

Physical Geography **61**
    Physical Geography Crossword Puzzle 62
    South American Rivers, Lakes, and Mountains Search 63
    South American Capital Matching 64
    Capital Map Exercise 64
    South American Capital Search 65

Demographics **66**
    Ranking World Cities by Population 66
    South American Cities Map Exercise 67
    Ranking South American Countries by Area 68
    Ranking South American Countries by Population 69

Maps **70**
    Map I: South America 70
    Map II: Climate Regions of South America 71
    Map III: Ocean and Wind Currents 72
    Map IV: Viceroyalties of South America 73
    Map V: Southern South America: Argentina and Chile 74
    Map VI: Brazil 75
    Map VII: Northern South America: Colombia, Venezuela, Guyana, Surinam, and French Guiana 76
    Map VIII: Ecuador, Peru, and Bolivia 77
    Map IX: Paraguay and Uruguay 78

Answer Keys **79**
Bibliography **92**

Introduction

Each continent is unique. Each has a historical record that includes a rare mixture of cultures from various parts of the world. South America is a continent where great Indian civilizations came face to face with European civilizations. However, continents include more than the cultures that have met, clashed, and often meshed. Mountains, ocean currents, latitude, rivers, and plains are only some of the features that make each continent special. In the pages of this book, you will be introduced to South America, a continent with a rich history and rich cultures.

Various map exercises throughout the book help students learn about the climates, physical features, and political boundaries of South America. Most of the maps are located in a separate section in the back of the book. Copies of these maps may be made as needed, since each map may be used in more than one activity. On maps that focus on specific countries, small maps of the entire continent have been included so students can see where these countries fit into the continent.

After an overview of the history, cultures, climates, and animals of South America, each country is profiled. Basic information, such as population, area, languages, religions, and date of independence, is included for each country. Also included is information on physical features, industries, agricultural products, climates, and natural resources. Panama has not been included in this book, since it may be considered a Central American country.

While South America is our neighbor in the Western Hemisphere, few people know much about its history, geography, and cultures. This book will help students gain valuable insight into this often overlooked, but richly fascinating, continent.

South America   Learning About Climates in South America

Name _____ Date _____

Learning About Climates in South America

   In studying the climates of South America, it is important to have an understanding of where the continent is located. Refer to Map I on page 70 and complete the following activity.

1. Draw a line on the map that shows the location of the equator. Label the line "equator."
2. Write the numeral 0° on each side of the word "equator" you have written on the line.

   The equator is an imaginary line that divides the earth into two halves. The northern half is the **Northern Hemisphere**, and the southern half is the **Southern Hemisphere**. **The equator is 0° latitude.**

3. Shade in the area north of the equator using ///////// symbols.

4. The countries of South America located in the shaded area are _____

_____

_____

   That part of the earth that is north of the equator is in the Northern Hemisphere. That part of the earth that is south of the equator is in the Southern Hemisphere.

5. The countries of South America that have **all** their territory in the Northern Hemisphere

are _____

_____

6. The countries of South America that have **all** their territory in the Southern Hemisphere

are _____

_____

_____

7. The countries of South America that have territory in both the Northern and Southern

Hemipsheres are _____

_____

© Mark Twain Media, Inc., Publishers

South America   Learning About the Tropics

Name _____ Date _____

LEARNING ABOUT THE TROPICS

That part of the earth's surface that is between the latitude lines of $23\frac{1}{2}°$ North and $23\frac{1}{2}°$ South is in the tropics. The latitude line of $23\frac{1}{2}°$ N is also called the **Tropic of Cancer**. The latitude line $23\frac{1}{2}°$ S is the **Tropic of Capricorn**. The importance of these two lines of latitude is the fact that the **direct rays of the Sun** are directly overhead somewhere between these two lines during the year. The direct rays are seen when the Sun is directly overhead at noon at a particular location.

Use a map or globe and answer the following questions.

1. The latitude of my location on the earth is _____ ° (North/South) of the equator.

2. I (will/will not) see the Sun **directly** overhead during the year at my latitude.

3. I (do/do not) live in the tropics.

Refer to the diagram below and shade in the region between $23\frac{1}{2}°$ N and $23\frac{1}{2}°$ S.

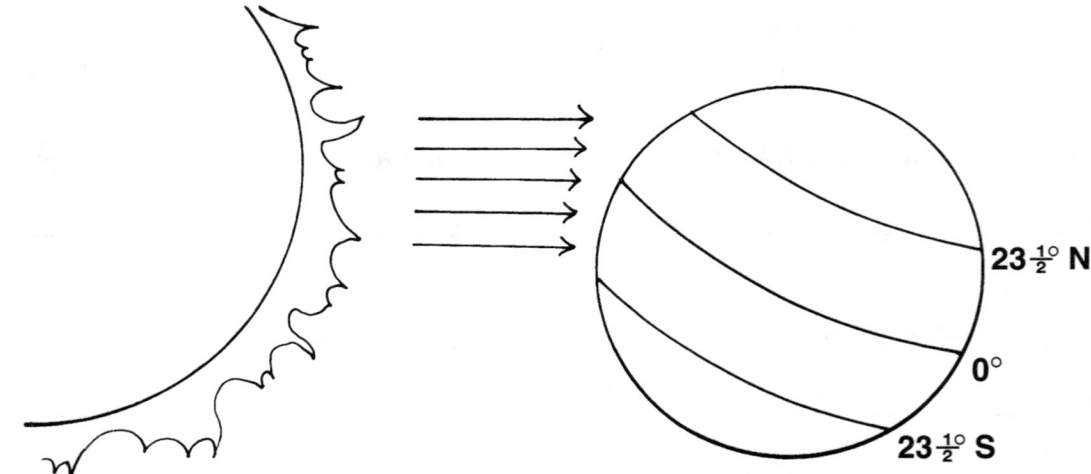

The curvature of the earth causes the Sun's rays to hit the earth at different angles at different latitudes on the earth. The area known as the tropics, located between $23\frac{1}{2}°$ N and $23\frac{1}{2}°$ S latitude, is the only region on earth that experiences the direct rays from the Sun. The direct rays appear overhead at noon at some latitude between these two lines of latitude each day during the year. Direct rays are those that strike the earth at an angle of 90 degrees. The direct rays strike the equator on two days of the year and at the Tropic of Cancer and the Tropic of Capricorn one day each year. The direct rays of the Sun strike the equator on March 21 and September 21. The direct rays strike the Tropic of Cancer ($23\frac{1}{2}°$ N) on June 21 and the Tropic of Capricorn ($23\frac{1}{2}°$ S) on September 21.

The movement of the direct rays from $23\frac{1}{2}°$ N to $23\frac{1}{2}°$ S and back to $23\frac{1}{2}°$ N takes one year. In this year, the direct rays strike the equator twice as the Sun crosses the equator.

South America   Learning About the Tropics

Name _____ Date _____

LEARNING ABOUT THE TROPICS (CONTINUED)

Refer to the map below and color the area between the dashed lines red. This is the tropical region.

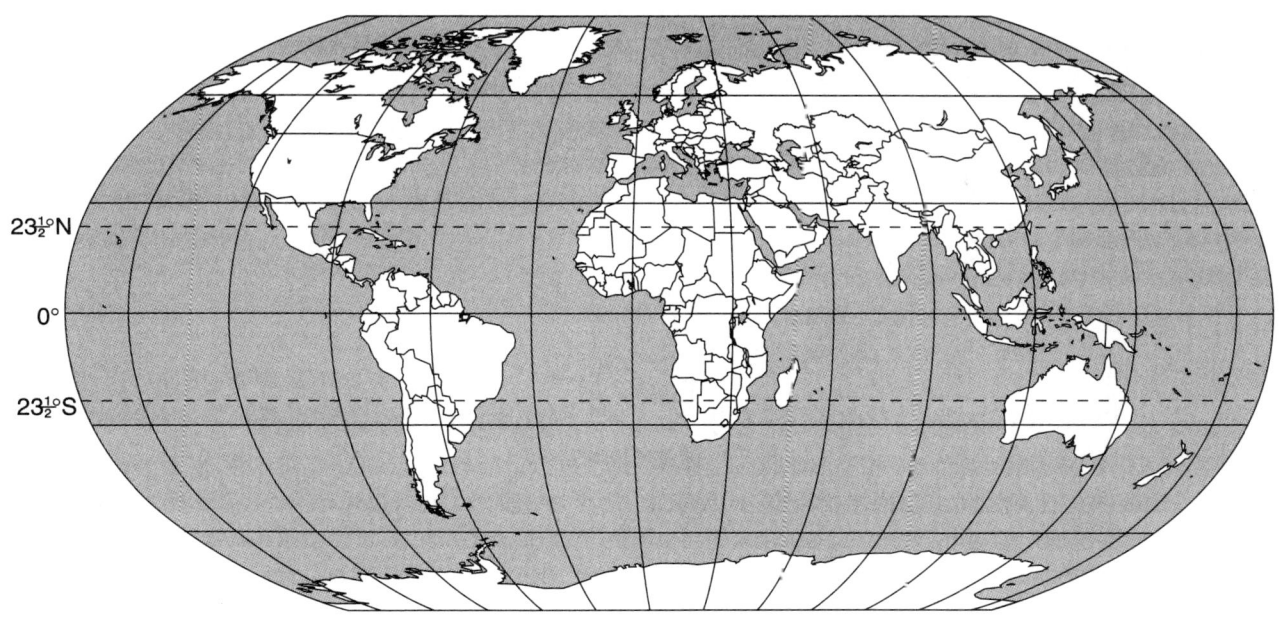

Refer to the map above and answer the following questions.

4. The nations of South America that are located completely in the tropics are:

_____

_____

5. The nations of South America that are located partially in the tropics are:

_____

The direct rays of the Sun are overhead sometime during the year at all locations in the tropics.

6. The following nations of South America will receive the direct rays of the Sun sometime

during the year: _____

_____

_____

LEARNING ABOUT THE SEASONS

The diagram below shows the path of the earth as it moves around the Sun during a year. The seasons are labeled for the Northern (N) and Southern (S) Hemispheres.

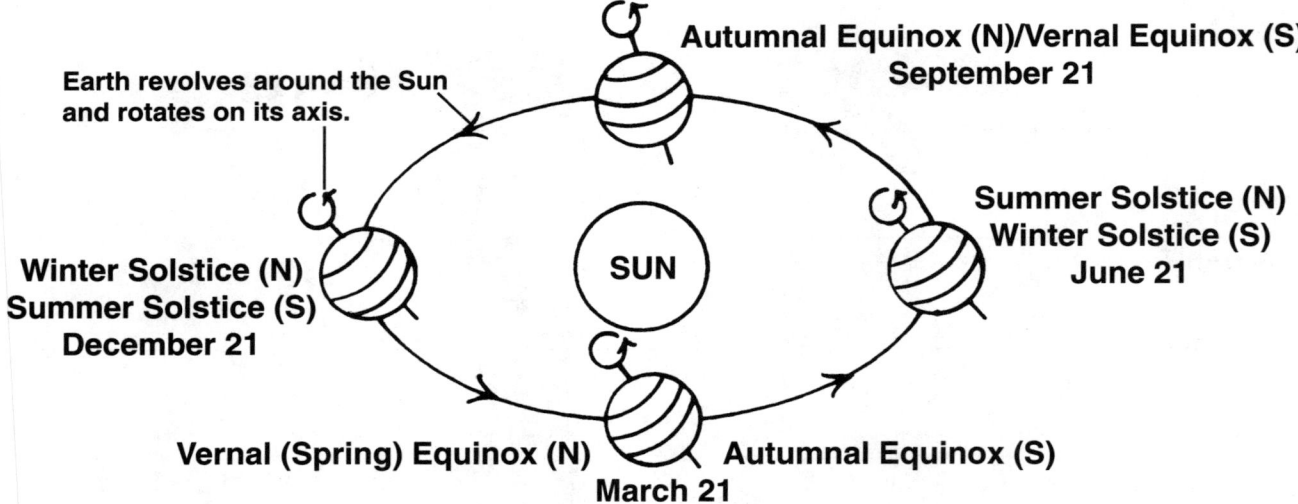

The earth makes one complete revolution around the Sun in a year. If the earth were not tilted on its axis, the seasons would be the same throughout the year. The tilt of the axis results in different parts of the earth facing the Sun at different times of the year. It is the revolution and tilt that creates the different seasons.

Refer to the above diagram and answer the following questions.

1. The _____ Hemisphere is tilted toward the Sun on June 21.
2. The _____ Hemisphere is tilted away from the Sun on June 21.
3. The _____ Hemisphere is tilted toward the Sun on December 21.
4. The _____ Hemisphere is tilted away from the Sun on December 21.
5. The earth is not tilted toward or away from the Sun on the dates _____ 21 and _____ 21.

Complete the blanks in the following selection using the terms below.

December   toward   **June**   away

The summer solstice in the Northern Hemisphere occurs on June 21. This is the longest daylight period in the Northern Hemisphere. In the Southern Hemisphere, it is the winter solstice, the shortest day or longest nighttime period in the Southern Hemisphere. The date of the winter solstice in the Southern Hemisphere is (6) _____ 21. The summer solstice in the Southern Hemisphere occurs on (7) _____ 21. The winter solstice in the Northern Hemisphere occurs on (8) _____ 21.

South America Learning About the Seasons

Name _____ Date _____

LEARNING ABOUT THE SEASONS (CONTINUED)

Summer in the Northern Hemisphere occurs when the Northern Hemisphere is tilted (9) _____ the Sun. Winter in the Northern Hemisphere occurs when the Northern Hemisphere is tilted (10) _____ from the Sun.

Summer in the Northern Hemisphere begins on (11) _____ 21 when the Northern Hemisphere is tilted toward the Sun. Winter in the Northern Hemisphere begins on (12) _____ 21 when the Northern Hemisphere is tilted away from the Sun.

Refer to the chart below and answer the questions that follow.

NORTHERN HEMISPHERE			
Autumn	**Winter**	**Spring**	**Summer**
September	December	March	June
October	January	April	July
Nobember	February	May	August
December	March	June	September
Spring	**Summer**	**Autumn**	**Winter**
SOUTHERN HEMISPHERE			

13. Summer in the Northern Hemisphere includes all or part of the months _____, _____, _____, and _____.
14. Winter in the Northern Hemisphere includes all or part of the months _____, _____, _____, and _____.
15. Summer in the Southern Hemisphere includes all or part of the months _____, _____, _____, and _____.
16. Winter in the Southern Hemisphere includes all or part of the months _____, _____, _____, and _____.
17. The Northern Hemisphere is having winter when the Southern Hemisphere is having _____.
18. The Northern Hemisphere is having summer when the Southern Hemisphere is having _____.

The fact that the seasons are reversed in the Northern and Southern Hemispheres is a result of the (19) _____ of the earth and the (20) _____ of the earth around the Sun.

© Mark Twain Media, Inc., Publishers

South America   Daylight and Darkness in the Tropics

Name _____ Date _____

DAYLIGHT AND DARKNESS IN THE TROPICS

One of the characteristics associated with areas in the tropics is that the periods of daylight and darkness in a 24-hour period are approximately equal.

Refer to the chart below and complete the blanks in the statements that follow. Read the chart for the Southern Hemisphere. The numbers to be used in the blanks are in bold below. In completing this exercise, note that the tropics are those areas between 23 $\frac{1}{2}°$ N and 23 $\frac{1}{2}°$ S latitude.

HOURS OF DAYLIGHT BY LATITUDE
(Hours and minutes on the 15th day of each month)

Northern Hemisphere Month	Equator	20°	50°	80°	Poles	Southern Hemisphere Month
JAN	12:07	11:02	8:30	0:00	0:00	JUL
FEB	12:07	11:21	10:07	0:00	0:00	AUG
MAR	12:07	12:00	11:48	10:52	0:00	SEP
APR	12:07	12:36	13:44	24:00	24:00	OCT
MAY	12:07	13:04	15:22	24:00	24:00	NOV
JUN	12:07	13:20	16:21	24:00	24:00	DEC
JUL	12:07	13:16	15:38	24:00	24:00	JAN
AUG	12:07	12:50	14:33	24:00	24:00	FEB
SEP	12:07	12:17	12:42	15:16	24:00	MAR
OCT	12:07	11:42	10:47	5:10	0:00	APR
NOV	12:07	11:12	9:06	0:00	0:00	MAY
DEC	12:07	10:56	8:05	0:00	0:00	JUN

10 hours, 56 minutes   **12 hours, 7 minutes**
8 hours, 5 minutes   **16 hours, 21 minutes**
0 hours, 0 minutes   **13 hours, 20 minutes**
24 hours, 0 minutes

1. Daylight hours for 0° _____ .
2. Daylight hours for 20° in the Southern Hemisphere range from _____ to _____ .
3. Daylight hours for 50° in the Southern Hemisphere range from _____ to _____ .
4. Daylight hours for 80° in the Southern Hemisphere range from _____ to _____ .
5. On the blanks below, explain why the daylight period varies so much at the higher latitudes.

_____

_____

© Mark Twain Media, Inc., Publishers

South America Temperature in the Tropics

Name _____ Date _____

TEMPERATURE IN THE TROPICS

Usually the tropics are areas where it is warm year-round. The tropical rain forest areas of the world are found here. The tropical rain forest is a region of dense forests, large amounts of rainfall, and year-round high temperatures.

However, not all areas of the tropics are rain forest areas. Those areas in the tropics that are in mountainous areas become cooler as one moves to the higher elevations. It also becomes drier and forest gives way to grasses. If the mountains are high enough, snow will also be present.

The diagram below is a mountain that is 12,000 feet high. **It is located on the equator**, a tropical area. "A" is a tropical city. The temperature at noon on a given day is 86°F at "A." Refer to the diagram and answer the questions that follow.

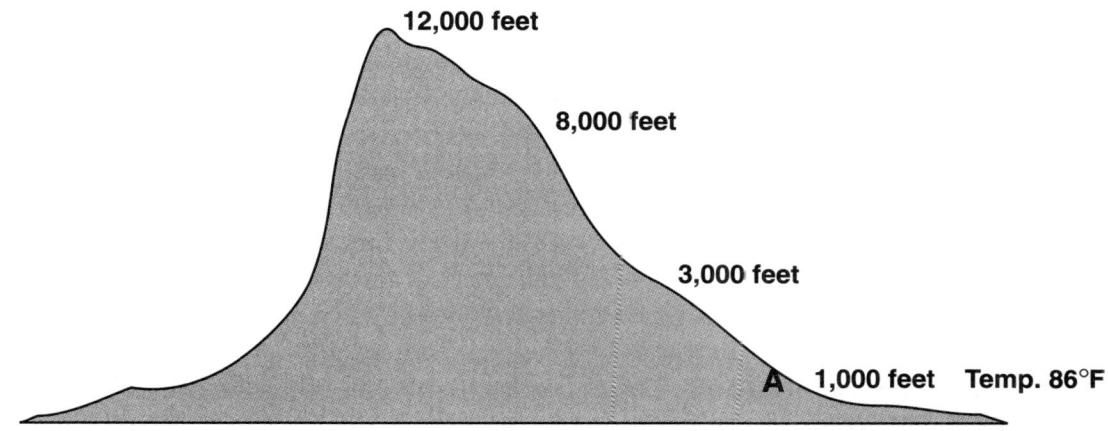

Assume that the temperature drops 3°F for every increase of 1,000 feet in elevation. Also assume that this mountain is in South America and Indian communities are located at 3,000 feet, 8,000 feet, and 12,000 feet.

1. The temperature in the community at 3,000 feet will be _____ °.
2. The temperature in the community at 8,000 feet will be _____ °.
3. The temperature in the community at 12,000 feet will be _____ °.
4. On the blanks below, explain how altitude affects temperature.

_____

_____

_____

_____

South America — Temperature in the Tropics

Name _____ Date _____

TEMPERATURE IN THE TROPICS (CONTINUED)

The climate of a South American country is influenced by its location within the tropics. Even though a country may have a tropical location, the climate is also influenced by its altitude. A city in the high Andes Mountains may have a very different climate than a city at the same latitude but closer to sea level.

Refer back to Map I and complete the following.

5. Draw mountain symbols ^ ^ ^ ^ on the map to locate the Andes Mountains.
6. Place a dot on the map to locate Manaus, Brazil. This city is located at a very low elevation level, close to sea level.
7. Place a dot on the map to locate Quito, Ecuador. This city is located in the high Andes Mountains at an elevation of 8,200 feet.

Both cities are located near the equator, a tropical location. However, Manaus is very hot and wet all year, while Quito is very cool and dry. In fact, not far above Quito is a high, snow-capped mountain.

8. The average monthly temperatures for Quito and Manaus are given below. Complete the line graph by placing a dot on the graph for each city's average monthly temperature. Connect the dots for Quito with a blue line, and connect the dots for Manaus with a red line. The dots for January have been placed for you.

Quito: January 58, February 59, March 59, April 59, May 59, June 59, July 57, August 59, September 59, October 59, November 58, December 59

Manaus: January 80, February 80, March 80, April 80, May 80, June 80, July 82, August 82, September 82, October 82, November 82, December 81

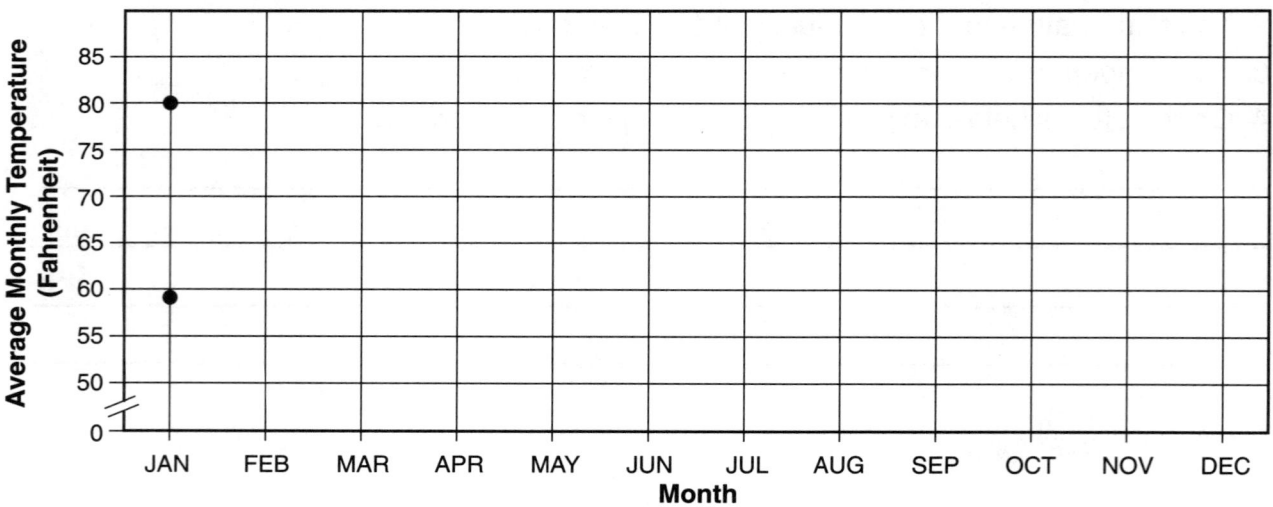

South America Temperature in the Tropics

Name _____ Date _____

Temperature in the Tropics (continued)

9. In your own words, explain why there is such a difference in climates between Manaus and Quito even though they are both located very close to the equator.

_____
_____
_____
_____
_____
_____
_____

In your study of South America, you will find that the altitude of a city, as well as the latitude, are very important in determining the type of climate that will be found. Later, you will find that ocean currents and prevailing winds also play a role in the type of climate found at a particular location.

10. Refer to the paragraph above and complete the graphic organizer below. Place the following terms in the ovals. The central idea should be placed in the middle oval, and the supporting ideas should be placed in the surrounding ovals.

ocean currents   latitude   climate   altitude   prevailing winds

You have found that not all countries in South America are located in the tropics. Refer to a map of South America and answer the following questions.

11. The island at the southern tip of South America is _____, which means "land of fire."

12. The latitude of this island is _____ ° S.

13. The island is located in the (Northern/Southern) Hemisphere.

South America   Climates in South America

Name _____ Date _____

Climates in South America

There are many climates in South America. The following are some of the major climate conditions found in South America. Read the description of the climate and then locate the climate on Map II. Complete the map activity that follows each climate description.

Tropical Rain Forest: The vegetation is tall trees forming a canopy over the ground below. The average temperature in all months is in the high 70s to low 80s. The highest temperature of the day may be in the 90s, with the lowest temperature in the 70s. Rainfall amounts are often 90 inches or more a year. The rainfall occurs throughout the year, with no dry season.

1. Refer to Map II and color the area marked "a" **red** to show where the tropical rain forest climate is found in South America.

Tropical Wet and Dry (Savanna): This climate in South America is found mostly in Brazil. It is located on the northern and southern borders of the tropical rain forest. This climate has definite wet and dry seasons. During the summer, the rain falls on most days and is often heavy. The winter season brings a long dry period when rivers and lakes become dry. The vegetation is largely grass, with trees in wetter areas. Rainfall amounts may vary, but in Brazil, at least 60 inches of rain falls each year. The average monthly temperatures are in the high 70s to low 80s.

2. Refer to Map II and color the areas marked "b" **pink** to show where the tropical wet and dry climate is found in South America.

Humid Subtropical: This climate is found in the Pampas region of Argentina. Rainfall comes throughout the year. Summers are usually wet and humid. The average summer temperature is usually in the 80s. Average winter temperatures are in the 40s. Along with the fertile soil, this climate type has been important in making the Pampas of Argentina one of the world's leading agricultural areas for grain crops like corn, soybeans, and wheat.

3. Refer to Map II and color the area marked "c" **green** to show where the humid subtropical climate is found in South America.

Mid-latitude Marine: The marine climate is found in Chile beginning at about 35° S and extending to the tip of Chile at Cape Horn. Summers are cool with average temperatures in the 60-degree range. Winters are mild with average temperatures in the 40s. Rainfall is distributed throughout the year and usually averages 30 to 40 inches per year. The cool temperatures throughout the year result in large forested areas. Lumbering is important in this climate.

4. Refer to Map II and color the area marked "d" **blue** to show where the mid-latitude marine climate is found in South America.

South America | Climates in South America

Name _____ Date _____

Climates in South America (continued)

Mediterranean: This climate in South America is found in the central valley of Chile. Summers are hot and dry. Winters are mild, and rainfall comes during the winter season. Average monthly winter temperatures are in the mid 50s. Average summer temperatures are in the 90s. The vegetation is often small, gnarled trees and shrubs with some grasses. This is the area of Chile where most of the citrus crops and small grains are raised.

5. Refer to Map II and color the area marked "e" **orange** to show where the Mediterranean climate is found in South America.

Desert: Desert climates occur in many regions of the world. Deserts may be cold or hot, but they are always dry. In some cases deserts are very hot during the day but become cold at night. Typically the vegetation is grass or very little vegetation. The rainfall per year is often less than ten inches. In South America, the Atacama is one of the driest deserts in the world. In many years, no rain falls. A narrow band of desert climate is found along the west coast of South America from Ecuador to northern Chile.

6. Refer to Map II and color the area marked "f" **brown** to show where the desert climate is found in South America.

Steppe (Semiarid): The steppe or semiarid climate is found in regions where the rainfall amount is only ten to 20 inches per year. The vegetation is usually grass. In this climate area, sheep and cattle are raised. Some years it is possible to raise grain crops. In years when the rain does not come, farmers and ranchers often face difficult times. In many semiarid areas, there are cool to cold winters and hot summers. The largest steppe climate in South America is found in Argentina in the Patagonia area.

7. Refer to Map II and color the area marked "g" **yellow** to show where the steppe/semiarid climate is found in South America.

Refer to the climate descriptions above and complete the following activity. Place a plus mark (+) in the rectangle if the word in that column is associated with that climate.

	Brazil	Argentina	Chile	Bolivia	Peru	West Coast	East Coast	Equator	Hot, Wet	Dry
8. Tropical Rain Forest										
9. Tropical Wet and Dry										
10. Humid Subtropical										
11. Mid-latitude Marine										
12. Mediterranean										
13. Desert										
14. Steppe/Semiarid										

© Mark Twain Media, Inc., Publishers

The Effects of Currents and Winds on Climate

Ocean currents often affect the climate of a region. There are two important features that help determine the effect the ocean current will have. One feature is whether the ocean current is a cold or warm current. The other feature is whether the winds moving across the current are blowing onshore or offshore.

An ocean current is a **cold current** when the temperature of the ocean current is cooler than the water the current is moving through. An ocean current is termed a **warm current** when the temperature of the current is warmer than the water the current is moving through. Typically, **cold currents flow from the direction of the poles** toward the equator and **warm currents flow from the direction of the equator** toward the poles.

Refer to Map III and locate the following currents. Indicate if the current is a warm or cold current.

1. Brazilian Current: (a) (warm/cold) current because it flows from the direction of the (b) (equator/pole).

2. Peruvian Current: (a) (warm/cold) current because it flows from the direction of the (b) (equator/pole).

An **onshore wind** is one that moves from over the water to the land. An **offshore wind** is one that moves from the land toward the water. When winds move across a warm current, the air mass picks up water vapor. When the air mass moves on shore, it cools and the water vapor changes to liquid and falls as rain. When the wind moves across a cool current, it does not pick up much moisture, so rainfall is not so likely on shore.

When air masses are forced over mountain ranges, the air mass cools and drops its moisture. The temperature of the air mass when it drops its moisture determines if the moisture will fall as rain or snow. If the air mass moves over a cold ocean current, it will have less moisture. It will be necessary for the air mass to reach a higher elevation before it drops its moisture. Therefore, when a cold ocean current is near a large land mass, the coastal area may be very dry. However, the nearby mountains may be snow-covered.

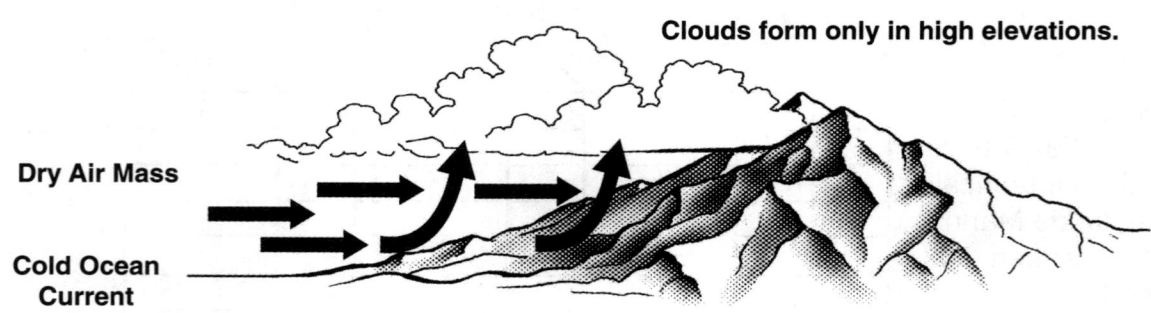

THE EFFECTS OF CURRENTS AND WINDS ON CLIMATE (CONTINUED)

Along the west coast of South America a cold current moves from the south pole north along the west coast toward the equator. This cold current is known as the **Peruvian Current**. This cold current brings plankton in large numbers to areas along the west coast. Since fish and other sea animals feed on the plankton, many people in the coastal areas make their living fishing.

Refer to Map III and complete the following activity.

3. Color the dashed line along the west coast of South America blue. This is the cool current that moves along the west coast of South America in most years.

4. The perpendicular dashed lines with arrows pointing toward Peru and Chile are westerly winds moving onshore. Trace over these dashed lines. These lines represent the air mass that moves onshore.

5. Since the winds are moving across a cool current, they do not pick up much moisture. Therefore, fog develops along the coast of Peru and Chile, but little rain falls. Write "fog" along the coast of Peru and Chile to indicate the influence of the cool current and westerly winds.

LEARNING ABOUT EL NIÑO

In some years, a strange thing happens. The Peruvian Current reverses and flows from the direction of the equator. This is a warm current rather than a cool one. When this happens, the plankton that the fish and sea animals live on do not appear. The fish and sea animals must leave the area to find cooler water or die. The fishermen face difficult times since there are no fish to catch.

When the ocean current reverses, the westerly winds moving across the warm current pick up large amounts of water vapor. When the wind hits the coast, the air mass is full of moisture and heavy rainfall occurs, rather than the usual fog. The heavy rainfall brings much flooding and destruction.

Long ago fishermen recognized that the warm current appears in some years. They also noted that this often happened around Christmas time. They named the warm current El Niño, which means "Christ Child" in Spanish.

Today, meteorologists recognize that the occurrence of El Niño upsets weather patterns around the world. When El Niño appears, places around the world that normally receive rainfall may become dry. Areas that are normally dry may become wet. The temperatures that would normally be expected in a region may not occur.

Refer to a new copy of Map III and complete the following activity.

1. Color the dashed line along the west coast of South America red. Change the arrows so they point south. This is the warm current that moves along the coast of South America in El Niño years.

2. Trace over the perpendicular lines with arrows pointing toward Peru and Chile. These represent westerly winds moving onshore.

Reviewing What I Have Learned

Complete the blanks in the following selection using the terms below.

El Niño   **plankton**   **warm current**   **cool current**   **fog**
rainfall   **fishermen**   **weather**   **Peruvian Current**   **flooding**

Normally there is a cool current off the coast of Chile, Peru, and Ecuador. This ocean current is called the (1) _____. When the westerly winds move onshore in Ecuador, Peru, and Chile, they do not contain much moisture, so (2) _____ develops rather than rainfall. The Peruvian Current is called a (3) _____ because it is cooler than the water it is passing through. The cool water brings lots of small sea animals called (4) _____, which fish and other sea animals eat. Because there are lots of fish in the cool water, many people from Ecuador, Peru, and Chile make a living as (5) _____ .

In some years, the Peruvian Current is replaced with a (6) _____ flowing from the direction of the equator. When this happens, the warm current is called an (7) _____ current. The plankton no longer appear, and the fish and sea animals leave the area or die. The westerly winds moving across the warm current pick up moisture, and when the winds move onshore, heavy (8) _____ occurs rather than fog. The heavy rainfall brings much (9) _____ and destruction to the normally dry coasts of Ecuador, Peru, and Chile. When the El Niño Current occurs, other parts of the world experience unusual (10) _____ patterns.

On the blanks below list some of the things you have learned about climate in South America.

11. _____
12. _____
13. _____
14. _____
15. _____
16. _____
17. _____
18. _____
19. _____
20. _____

A Historical Look at the South American Population

EUROPEAN

In the early 1500s, Spanish and Portuguese explorers turned their attention to the Americas. The Spanish were exploring and conquering the lands of Central America and South America. The Portuguese exploration was limited to that part of South America that is now Brazil. Many of these explorers were common men who had come to the new world in hopes of becoming rich. They had heard stories of the Indian civilizations and the riches that might be obtained. When the Europeans came in contact with the native Indians, they often heard stories about gold and precious metals that these civilizations possessed. One famous myth was that of El Dorado. The myth of El Dorado was that there existed an Indian leader who covered himself with gold dust throughout the year. Then, once each year he would dive into a pool and wash the gold from his body. Myths like this drove the conquistadors to face untold hardships to find El Dorado.

The Spanish were aggressive in exploring and conquering the lands of South America. Conquistador means "conquerer" in Spanish. The Spanish conquistadors usually consisted of small groups, but with armor and horses, a small force of Europeans was able to conquer an entire Indian civilization.

Portugal and Spain were competing to conquer and control South America. The issue was finally solved with the signing of the Treaty of Tordesillas. This treaty, signed by Spain and Portugal in 1494, gave Portugal the right to explore and conquer the land up to a line 370 leagues west of the Azores Islands. That is approximately 50° West longitude. The result was that Portugal was given access to the land that is Brazil today. Brazil was ruled by Portugal until 1822, when it gained its independence. However, the Portuguese language is still spoken in Brazil, and the culture is rich in Portuguese traditions.

While Portugal was exploring and conquering Brazil, the Spanish conquistadors were conquering the rest of South America. The Spanish imposed their culture on the land conquered. Today, Spanish is a major language spoken in the South American countries of Venezuela, Colombia, Peru, Ecuador, Bolivia, Chile, Paraguay, Argentina, and Uruguay.

Spanish Conquistadors

Francisco Pizarro

Francisco Pizarro was the son of a nobleman and a common woman in Spain. While living in Spain, he was a swineherder. He became part of Balboa's group that came to the Americas exploring Panama. Pizarro was one of the first Europeans to see the Pacific Ocean. While exploring in Central America, he heard stories from natives that far to the south was a land of riches where gold was common. Uneducated and without money, he went back to Spain and finally secured ships and financial support from the king and queen of Spain.

When Pizarro entered what is now Peru with his Spanish soldiers, he found that there was a civil war going on in the Inca Empire. Atahualpa and Huascar, the two sons of the last great Inca, Huanyna Capac, were fighting each other. The civil war ended with Atahualpa winning.

Pizarro and his companions then defeated the Incas and sacked Cuzco, the Incan capital. In Cuzco they found gold and sent it back to the king in Spain. From this point, South America became a source of gold bullion for Spanish kings to finance the wars that Spain was involved in back in Europe.

Pedro de Valdivia

Once the Spanish had conquered Peru and Bolivia, their attention turned to Chile. Pedro de Valdivia was the conquistador who led the exploration into Chile. In Chile the Spaniards faced the Araucanian Indians. These were fierce Indians who resisted the Spanish for many years. Valdivia lost his life trying to bring the Araucanians under the control of the Spanish. Many years were to pass and many conflicts between the Spanish and Araucanians were to occur before the land was brought under the control of the Spanish.

Portuguese

Pedro Alvarez Cabral

Pedro Alvarez Cabral claimed Brazil for Portugal in 1500. History records that while sailing from Lisbon, Portugal, seeking a route to India, Cabral was blown off course. After being blown off course, Cabral and his crew sighted a promontory and, upon landing, claimed the land for Portugal. Many believe that Cabral had heard stories of the land of Brazil and was not blown off course, but that he was actively looking for this new land.

South America   A Historical Look at the South American Population: Incas

Name _____ Date _____

INDIANS OF SOUTH AMERICA

INCAS

    In the high Andes, Indian civilizations had developed to a high level. The last of the Indian civilizations was the Incas. This great civilization extended from what is now northern Ecuador south to what is now the middle of Chile—a distance of 2,500 miles. The empire extended from the Pacific Coast on the west to the Amazon jungle on the east.

    On the map below, color in the area marked with dashes to show the extent of the Inca Empire.

© Mark Twain Media, Inc., Publishers   18

INCAS (CONTINUED)

The Inca Empire was ruled by the **Inca** or Great Ruler. The Lord Inca traveled throughout the empire in a curtained litter with a number of warriors for protection. The male members of the royal family could be recognized by their ear lobes, which almost touched their shoulders. The large ear lobes were a result of objects that were placed in the ear lobe when the royal males were very young. The objects were worn over a long period of time and increased in size until the ear lobes stretched to the desired length.

The Incas worshipped the Sun. Gold was common in the temples and was recast in the shape of the Sun, animals, fountains, and jewelry. It was the stories of the gold that the conquistadors heard in Central America that encouraged men like Pizarro and Valdivia to face many hardships and risk their lives in hopes of becoming rich.

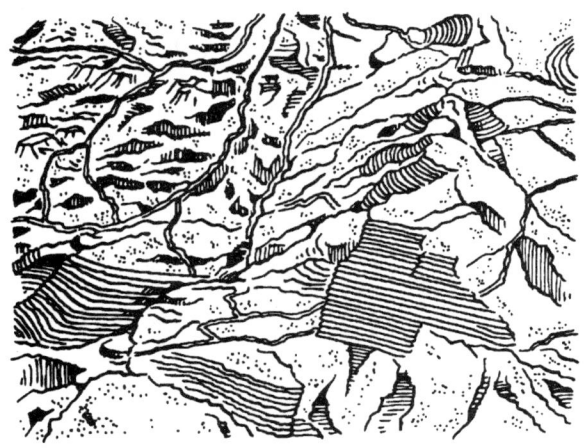

The city of Cuzco in Peru was the first settlement of the Incas. This city was located at an elevation of 10,000 feet near Lake Titacaca on the Bolivian Plateau. The Incas grew corn and potatoes on terraces they built on the mountains. Stones were used to make walls on the mountains, and then soil was filled in behind the stone wall to form a field for raising crops.

In addition to the terraces, the Incas built great stone structures. One of the most famous is at Machu Picchu in Peru. Here the Incas built great buildings from huge stones that they had carved to fit tightly together. These structures still stand today, long after the Inca Empire has disappeared. Today no one is sure how the Incas were able to move these huge stones to the location high in the Andes and fit them together so tightly.

The Incas were skilled craftsmen. Pottery making, weaving, and gold working were highly developed skills. Even today the skills of the Incas are evident in the pottery and weaving of the Indians of the Andes.

Several animals were domesticated by the Incas. The **alpaca** was used as a beast of burden, and the **vicuña** was raised for its wool. From the vicuña's wool the Incas made beautiful cloths with many bright colors and elaborate designs.

INCAS (CONTINUED)

The Incas were also great astronomers. They studied the stars and developed a very accurate calendar based on twelve months. The calendar was very important in their daily life and it was used to determine when religious ceremonies would take place.

The religion of the Incas placed great emphasis on the Sun and its location at different times of the year. The location of the Sun signified the time to plant crops like corn. The planting season was a time of great religious ceremony when the Incas prayed to the Sun god.

Land in the Inca Empire was owned communally. Individuals did not own land. It  belonged to the community. The main crops were maize (corn) and potatoes. The crops were stored to be used by everyone. The Incas had developed a system for distributing the stored food so that no one would go hungry.

To hold the empire together, the Incas developed an elaborate road system that extended to all parts of the empire. Messages and goods were delivered from one part of the empire to another by runners who were stationed at various points along the roadway. The runners were known as **chasquis**. Chasquis were stationed very close together so that they could run rapidly to the next station. Using this method, the chasquis could move a message approximately 150 miles per day.

The Incas kept records and sent messages by using a **quipu**. The quipu was a series of colored strings bound together. Messages were recorded on the quipu using the colored strings. The quipu was important in running the empire since all records were kept using this tool.

The language spoken by the Incas was known as **Quechan**. It is still spoken by some Indians in the highlands of Bolivia and Peru.

South America   Incas: Reviewing What I Have Learned

Name _____ Date _____

REVIEWING WHAT I HAVE LEARNED

Read the following selection. Fill in the blanks with one of the words or phrases below. Some terms are used more than one time.

Cuzco	terraces	Peru	conquistadors	Inca
Chile	Great Ruler	Bolivia	Machu Pichu	colors
craftsmen	Sun	roads	calendar	gold
quipu	civil	chasquis	Quechan	designs

When the Spanish (1) _____ arrived in South America, a great Indian civilization was found in the high Andes. The Indian civilization was the (2) _____ Empire. The Inca's were ruled by the Inca or (3) _____ . The capital of the Inca Empire was located near the present-day city of (4) _____ . Today, there are ruins such as the ones at (5) _____ that show the great building skill of the Incas.

The language spoken by the Incas was (6) _____ . It was spoken by over five million Incas throughout the empire. Today, the language is still spoken by large numbers of Indians in the highlands of the Andes.

The Incas built (7) _____ on the mountain sides to raise fields of maize and potatoes. All of the land in the empire was owned by the community. The food raised was shared by all members of the empire.

The Inca Empire extended in the north from the present-day country of (8) _____ , to the south through the high plateau located in (9) _____ , to what is now central (10) _____ .

All parts of the empire were connected by a system of (11) _____ that made it possible to travel throughout the empire in a short period of time. The runners who lived in huts near the highway and carried the messages throughout the empire were called (12) _____ .

The Incas worshipped the (13) _____ and placed great emphasis on its location at various time of the year. To help them determine the location of the Sun, they developed a (14) _____ with a twelve-month year.

They were very skilled (15) _____ and made elaborate ornaments out of (16) _____ . The stories of this (17) _____ encouraged the Spanish (18) _____ to invade the Inca Empire.

Records were kept by using a string called a (19) _____ . This item had strings of different (20) _____ . The recording system was based on knots in a string and the color of the string.

© Mark Twain Media, Inc., Publishers

DISCUSSION QUESTIONS

To the Teacher: The following are suggested questions for class discussion following the study of the Incas. It is not suggested that these questions be used for testing or grading. The purpose of the questions is to have students engage in discussion that requires them to think.

1. What was the name of the great Indian empire Pizarro found in what is now Peru and Bolivia? (low-level fact question)

2. What did the Incas use the alpaca for? (low-level fact question)

3. What are some gardening or farming techniques developed by the Incas that could be used today? (application question)

4. What can be learned about maintaining a successful empire from the experience of the Incas? (application question)

5. Why was the Inca Empire so successful? (analysis question)

6. How did the location in the Andes Mountains help the Inca civilization develop to this high level of sophistication? (analysis question)

7. Why was Pizarro, with only a small force, able to defeat the Incas, who numbered in the thousands? (synthesis question)

8. Why did the rulers of Spain finance the expeditions of the conquistadors? (synthesis question)

9. If you had been the Great Inca, what would you have done to keep Pizarro from succeeding in capturing the empire? (evaluation question)

10. What are some things about the Inca Empire that indicate it was a sophisticated civilization? (evaluation question)

INDIANS OF THE AMAZON

When Cabral landed in what is now Brazil, he was met by Indians. These Indians were far different from the Incas. The Indians of the Amazon had learned to survive in the hot, rainy conditions found in the rain forest. Due to the high temperatures and rainfall throughout the year, the rain forest was the home of many animals and plants.

The Indians of the Amazon raised some of their food, but they also depended on hunting, fishing, and finding edible plants. The Indians practiced a **"slash-and-burn" type of agriculture**. The vegetation on a plot of ground was cut down and burned. The ashes provided some fertilizer, but after a few years, the soil became depleted of the nutrients needed to produce crops. When this happened, the tribe moved to a new area and again cleared it by burning. They again moved on a few years later. Crops raised included corn, yams, manioc, peanuts, and bananas. Where the Incas had developed a large empire with thousands of citizens, the Indians of the Amazon lived in small, self-sufficient tribes.

Today, Indians living in the Amazon region are more dependent on farming than on hunting, fishing, and gathering. Some have taken jobs on plantations or in towns. Although many tribes still retain practices from the past, their way of life has changed as the Indians have come in contact with the modern world.

ARAUCANIAN INDIANS

When Pedro de Valdivia came to explore what is today Chile, he found the land inhabited by the Araucanian Indians. These Indian warriors refused to submit to the Spanish conquistadors. The Araucanians fought the Spanish for many years, but they were eventually defeated by the Spanish. However, rather than submit to the Spanish, many of the Araucanians crossed the Andes into Argentina.

Once in Argentina, their society was built around hunting, fishing, and raising crops. After obtaining horses, the Araucanians maintained a way of life somewhat like various tribes of plains Indians in North America. Today, some still live on reservations and maintain their cultural identity. Others have chosen to live off of the reservation and become part of the dominant culture.

South America   Amazonian and Araucanian Indians: Reviewing What I Have Learned

Name _____ Date _____

Reviewing What I Have Learned

Use the words below to complete the blanks in the following selection about the Indians of the Amazon.

slash-and-burn	**modern**	**hunting**	**yam**	**fishing**
manioc	**plantations**	**advanced**	**infertile**	**Inca**

When Cabral discovered Brazil, he found Indian tribes living in the Amazon area. These Indians lived primarily by (1) _____, (2) _____, and gathering edible plants from the forest. The agriculture they practiced was called (3) _____. This meant that a plot of ground would be cleared and burned and crops would be planted. After a few years, the soil would become (4) _____, and the Indians would select a new plot to grow crops.

Gradually, agriculture became more important to the tribes of the Amazon. They began to raise crops, including (5) _____, also called cassava, a tropical plant raised for its starchy root. The root is pounded into a pulp that is an important source of food. A crop like the sweet potato, also raised for its root, is the (6) _____.

The tribes in the Amazon never developed an (7) _____ civilization like the (8) _____ Empire in the Andes. However, influenced by the (9) _____ world, many of the tribal members today work on (10) _____.

Use the words below to complete the blanks in the following selection about the Araucanian Indians.

Chile	**conquistador**	**plains**	**Araucanians**	**Argentina**
reservations	**cultural**	**warrior**	**Andes**	**North America**

When the Spanish (1) _____, Valdivia, explored (2) _____, he found many Indian tribes. He was able to defeat most of the tribes, except for the (3) _____. This (4) _____ tribe refused to submit to the Spanish conquistador. Many of the Araucanians crossed the (5) _____ into (6) _____. There they lived much like some of the (7) _____ Indians of (8) _____.

Today, some descendants of the Araucanians have chosen to become part of the general society of Argentina and Chile. However, some have chosen to live on (9) _____ and maintain their (10) _____ identity.

South America | South America Under Spain's Rule

Name _____ Date _____

South America Under Spain's Rule

Once the conquistadors had defeated the Indians, the Spanish crown divided the continent into **viceroyalties**. Then each of the viceroyalties was placed under the control of a Spanish **viceroy** selected by the king of Spain. The Spanish king looked at South America as a place to enrich the coffers of Spain. It was the job of the viceroys to collect gold and silver and send it back to Spain.

The viceroyalties were further divided into large parcels of land and granted to other Spaniards. These large estates were called **encomendas**. These large estates required a large labor force, so the Indians and **Mestizos** (people of mixed ancestry, such as Spanish and Indian) who lived on the encomendas were forced to work for the owners. The work was hard, and the Indians and Mestizos were treated as serfs. The owners of the large estates had to pay taxes, which were sent back to Spain. The owners then taxed the Indians and Mestizos.

The harsh treatment of the Indians and Mestizos finally resulted in uprisings in various viceroyalties. The uprisings were put down in a very brutal fashion, and many of the natives lost their lives.

SPANISH RULE MAP EXERCISE

Refer to Map IV on page 73 and complete the following activity.

1. Color each of the viceroyalties a different color.

2. How many viceroyalties existed in South America? _____

3. List the viceroyalties under Spain's control. _____

_____

_____

South America Gains Independence

The South American countries were ruled by viceroys for almost three hundred years following the victories of the conquistadors. The viceroys were the king of Spain's representatives in the new world. These men were to provide Spain with the riches that could be wrested from the land.

The Indians and Mestizos were kept in bondage by the viceroys and were forced to work in the silver, gold, and copper mines. Many other Spaniards owned large land estates on which livestock and other foods were produced. Indians and Mestizos who lived on these estates were forced to work for the land owners.

By the year 1800, many of the people in South America were aware of the American Revolutionary War and the fact that the United States had gained independence from England. These individuals felt that the South American nations should not be ruled by Spain. Men like **Simón Bolívar**, who liberated Venezuela, Colombia, Ecuador, and Peru, and **José de San Martín**, who led a military force against Spain in Argentina, Chile, and Peru, led the fight for independence in South America.

Simón Bolívar, known as the "George Washington of South America," was a Creole living in the viceroyalty that includes what is now Venezuela. A **Creole** was a person born in South America to European parents. Europeans born in Spain felt they were at a higher social level than the Creoles. Creoles were often wealthy, but they felt those Europeans who had been born in Spain did not give them the opportunities they deserved.

Once independence was gained, men like Bolívar became the presidents of the new nations. However, often these same men felt that the people of South America were not capable of self-government. When the constitutions were written for the newly-independent nations, the leaders were made president for life. The poor people who had supported the leaders in the fight for independence did not gain the rights that they felt they had been fighting for.

People soon became unhappy with the results of their new independence. When this happened, revolutions occurred. The revolutions were often led by military leaders who gained control of the country and became dictators. For many years, the nations of South America were ruled by dictators who were frequently overthrown and replaced by yet another set of dictators.

BRAZIL

Brazil did not experience the same revolutions and unrest that came to exist in the South American countries controlled by Spain. Because of unrest in Europe during Napoleon's reign in France and the weakened condition of Portugal, the royalty of Portugal came to live in Brazil in 1808. This was a far different situation than what existed in the countries controlled by Spain. No Spanish king or queen ever set foot in the countries of South America that they controlled.

There was a desire for independence in Brazil. Many of the people were poor and lived under dire circumstances. However, the revolution did not occur as it did in other South American countries. There was no Bolívar or San Martín to lead a great revolt in Brazil. Instead, pressures for change in the way the royal family led Brazil were gradual, and as gradual changes were made, Brazil gained independence without a great revolution.

Spanish Rule and Independence Crossword Puzzle

Use the clues below to complete the crossword puzzle. Answers may be found in the information about the Spanish rule of South America and the independence of South American countries.

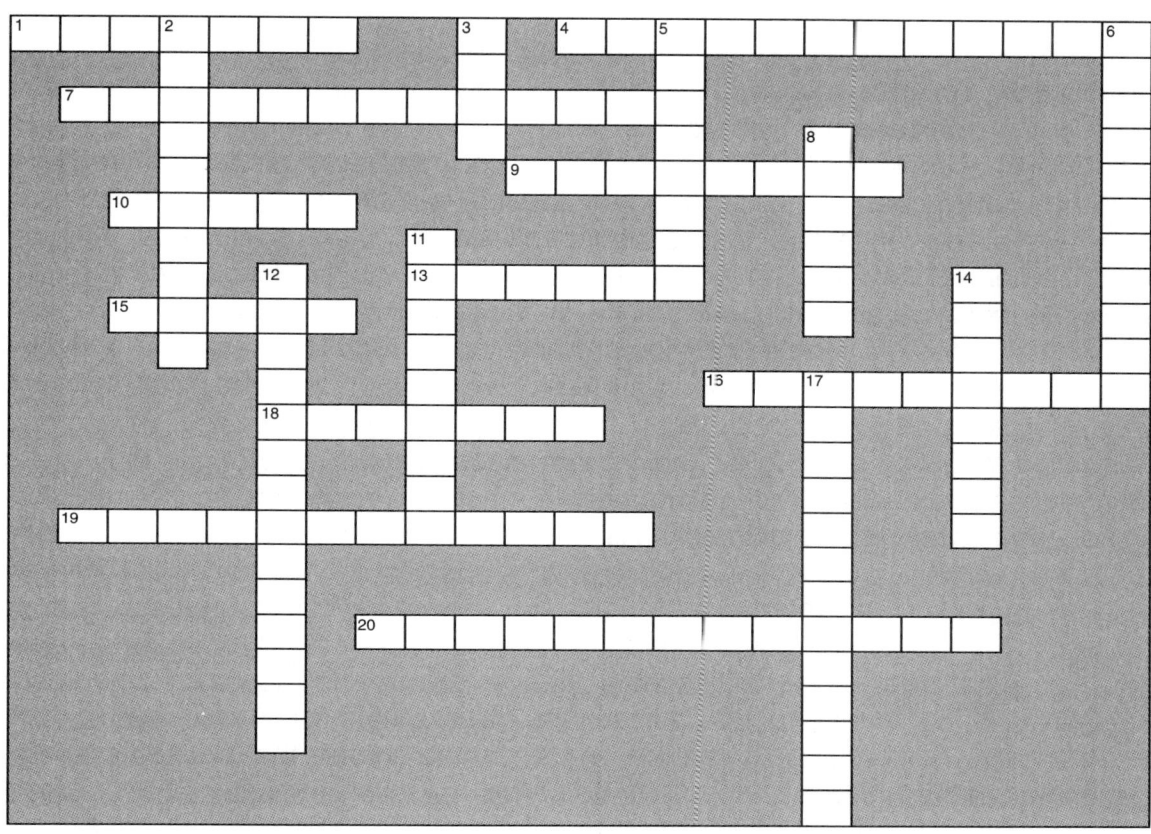

ACROSS
1. The representative of the king of Spain
4. The "George Washington of South America" (two words)
7. South America was divided into _____, each under the control of a representative of the king.
9. José de San Martín led a _____ force against the Spanish.
10. Indians and Mestizos were treated as _____.
13. Poor people did not gain the _____ they had expected when they fought for independence.
15. The owners of large estates had to pay _____ to Spain.
16. For many years, the nations of South America were ruled by _____.
18. Brazil gained independence as _____ changes were made.
19. People in South America heard about the _____ _____ gaining its independence from England.
20. Creoles were not given the same _____ as those who were European-born.

DOWN
2. Large estates granted to Spaniards
3. It was expected that _____ and silver would be sent back to Spain.
5. People of mixed ancestry
6. People unhappy with the results of their new independence started _____.
8. A person born in South America to European parents
11. Constitutions for the newly-independent nations made their leaders _____ for life.
12. Bolívar and other leaders thought the people were not capable of _____.
14. The royalty of _____ came to live in Brazil in 1808.
17. Spanish _____ defeated the native Indians of South America.

Animals of South America

South America is home to many animals and insects. There are animals and insects that are unlike those found in other parts of the world. Birds and butterflies abound with beautiful colors and unique plumage. The following are examples of the unique animals found in South America.

Monkeys are one of the most fascinating animals found in South America. They are different than the monkeys from other parts of the world. They are usually much smaller and live in the tropical areas, where they are found living in the trees. There are many different types of monkeys in South America, each type having special characteristics. One of the unique characteristics for some species is a prehensile tail. Those with the prehensile tail can wrap the tail around branches and hang without using their other limbs. There are other monkeys that have very short tails that cannot be used to seize tree limbs. Some of the monkeys are extremely small—only a few inches in length.

Sloths, anteaters, and armadillos are common in South America. The **sloth** is a slow-moving animal that lives in the rain forest. Even though they are very slow-moving animals, sloths are very hard for other animals to kill. Some of their protection is a result of a sharp claw found on each foreleg. They are also difficult to spot since they make no sudden moves and easily blend into their environment. In addition to its slow-moving behavior, another characteristic of the sloth is its tendency to hang upside down on the limbs of trees.

Anteaters are found in and around tropical forests. Their main food is termites found in the forest and in the drier lands outside the tropical forest. Like many other animal species, there are different types of anteaters. Some live in the trees, others live in the trees and on the ground, and some live on the ground outside the forested areas.

The **armadillo** is most famous for its hard shell that serves like armor. When attacked, the armadillo rolls up in a ball so the hard shell serves  as protection. The meat of the armadillo is very tasty and is often eaten by humans. Armadillos are found in many areas of South America. They are common in Argentina and Brazil.

One of the most interesting animals found in South America is the **tapir**. The tapir is a large, pig-like animal that weighs 300 to 500 pounds when full grown. The tapir lives on land, but it is very comfortable in the water. In fact, tapirs are almost always found living near a stream. When threatened, the tapir finds safety by escaping into a stream or lake.

A group of animals related to the camel are also found in South America. These are the **alpaca**, **vicuña**, **guanaco**, and **llama**. The guanaco are found in herds in the Pampas region of Argentina, while the alpaca, llama, and vicuña are found in mountainous regions. The alpaca, llama, and vicuña were domesticated by the Inca Indians. The alpaca is a beast of burden that is very sure-footed in the mountains and capable of carrying a large load. Llamas and vicuña are raised primarily for their fine wool and meat.

The **Patagonia** region of Argentina has become famous as a place where ancient animal life once existed. **Dinosaur bones**, along with the bones and evidence of other extinct animals, have been found in Patagonia.

South America — Animals of South America: Reviewing What I Have Learned

Name _____ Date _____

REVIEWING WHAT I HAVE LEARNED

Refer to the reading selection on page 28 and complete the following blanks.

This animal found in South America lives mainly in the tropical forests. Some of the types of this animal hang from tree limbs using their prehensile tails. Other members of this animal group are very small, being only a few inches long. The animals described are all (1) _____ .

This is the region of South America where animals that are now extinct once roamed. (2) _____ bones have been found here. This region is (3) _____, located in the nation of (4) _____ .

These animals of South America are related to the camel. The animals are the (5) _____, (6) _____, (7) _____, and (8) _____. These are domesticated animals. The (9) _____ is used as a beast of burden, while the (10) _____ and (11) _____ are raised for their (12) _____ and meat.

The (13) _____ has a very hard shell that serves to protect it from predators. When a predator approaches, this animal rolls up in a (14) _____ so it is protected by its shell.

An animal that lives near streams or lakes is the (15) _____ . When an enemy approaches, this animal will immediately run to get safely into the (16) _____ . This animal is somewhat like a hippopotamus, since it forages on (17) _____ for food, but spends a great deal of time in the water.

The (18) _____ is a very slow-moving animal. Because it is so slow-moving, it is often attacked by enemies, but it protects itself with its forelegs, each of which have a sharp (19) _____ . Even when hurt, this animal can stand a great deal of pain and still survive. This animal can also hang upside down from the limbs of (20) _____ .

Locating and Identifying South American Animals

Locate the following on the map at right. Place the letters in parentheses beside each animal on the map to show locations where that animal might be found.

Extinct animal bones (db db)
Sloths (sl sl)
Tapirs (tp tp)
Monkeys (mk mk)
Alpaca (al al)
Vicuña (vc vc)
Guanacos (gu gu)
Llamas (ll ll)
Armadillos (ar ar)
Anteaters (ant ant)

The following are other animals or insects found in South America. Use any resource you choose to find out where these animals and insects live and as much about their characteristics as you can. Use your own paper to list the information you find.

Birds:

1. Oropendolas
2. Manakins
3. Motmot
4. Hummingbirds

Snakes:

5. Anacondas
6. Jararaca

Insects:

7. Caligo
8. Click Beetles

Holidays and Festivals

In South America the people celebrate many holidays and festivals. The activities for each holiday or festival differ from country to country. Most include religious activities as well as celebrations that include music, dancing, and food. Many of the holidays and festivals can be traced to Spain, Portugal, and the Catholic religion. However, the activities include traditions from the Native Indian and African American cultures that exist along with the cultural influence of Spain and Portugal.

In Paraguay **the Fiesta of the Three Kings** in Tobati is celebrated on January 6 with a Mass and procession of the saints. The procession is escorted by a camba, or small band. Clowns dance, joke, and play musical instruments, such as flutes, as the procession moves along. This festival is enjoyed by everyone, but it is particularly important to the young people. There are games like climbing a greased pole, bow and arrow shooting contests, and games on horseback, as well as races. Young people can win prizes that include food and money.

Paraguay and Peru celebrate June 24 as **St. John's Day** or **the Fiesta de San Juan**. It is a time of merriment and fun that is special for young, unmarried girls. During the festival, the young girls perform various rituals, trying to find out something about when and whom they might marry. For example, one ritual calls for a girl to throw a shoe over a house. If the shoe lands upside down, the thrower will not marry within the next year.

The Saturday before Ash Wednesday marks the beginning of **Carnival** in Brazil. Carnival is celebrated with dancing, beginning late in the evening and continuing until daybreak. Each night Brazilians dress in elaborate costumes, often with masks, and attend costume balls. Carnival is celebrated throughout Brazil in each community.

The period from June 13 to June 29 finds the Brazilians celebrating **the Festas Juninas**. There are town processions followed by singing, dancing, and plays, like the folk drama Bumba-mew-Boi.

A special holiday for Peruvians is **Palm Sunday**. It is **the Fiesta da Ramos in Moche**. Peruvians begin the festival by attending a special Mass. Following the Mass, there is music, dancing, and food for enjoyment. Popular foods for this festive occasion include cabrito, yucca, and sweet potatoes.

In Argentina, Chile, Paraguay, and Peru, **the Day of the Holy Cross** is observed. This holiday commemorates the discovery of the cross on which Jesus was crucified. Crosses are decorated and displayed along roads and in the communities.

Although the day of celebration may vary from country to country, the **Christmas** season is a very special time in South America. Traditions, such as manger scenes similar to those found in the United States, are common. In each country, special Masses are held during the Christmas period. There are celebrations that include gift exchanges, dancing, music, and special activities for the young.

South America — Holidays and Festivals: Reviewing What I Have Learned

Name _____ Date _____

REVIEWING WHAT I HAVE LEARNED

For each of the following holidays or festivals, tell where the event is celebrated, when it is celebrated, and how it is celebrated.

1. Fiesta of the Three Kings: _____
_____
_____
_____

2. Carnival: _____
_____
_____
_____

3. Fiesta de Ramos in Moche: _____
_____
_____
_____

4. Day of the Holy Cross: _____
_____
_____
_____

5. Festas Juninas: _____
_____
_____
_____

6. St. John's Day: _____
_____
_____
_____

© Mark Twain Media, Inc., Publishers

Countries of South America Today

ARGENTINA

Area: 1,068,296 sq. miles
Population: 34,663,000; European 85%, Mestizo or Amerindian 15%
Major Religion: Roman Catholic
Major Language: Spanish
Independence: 1816

Just as Chile is a long, narrow country extending 2,600 miles from north to south, Argentina, its neighbor to the east, is a long, broad country with many climates. The high Andes Mountains on the border with Chile, the broad, fertile, flat land known as the Pampas, the subtropical areas of towering forest near Paraguay, and the Patagonian plateau make Argentina a unique country.

In Argentina, the major language spoken is Spanish. Most of the people are located in the city of Buenos Aires. Argentina is a nation with a definite European air. Approximately 85 percent of the population is of European extraction, mainly German, Italian, and Spanish.

The **Chaco**, a subtropical region in northern Argentina, is an area of forest with large trees. The leaves from the yerba tree are used to make a green tea called Yerba Mate. The Chaco is home to the famous quebracho and lapacho trees. The quebracho tree, known as the "axe breaker," is very hard. However, it yields lumber and tannin, a substance used in the tanning of leather. The lapacho tree is also very hard, beautiful, and resistant to decay. It has been widely used in buildings.

The **Pampas** (grassy plain) is a vast fertile plain in Argentina. This is one of the world's most productive agriculture regions. Large livestock ranches and grain farms, producing crops like wheat, corn, and soybeans, are found here.

Patagonia is a dry, cold, windy, and desolate plateau area in southern Argentina.

The high, rugged **Andes Mountains** form the western border between Chile and Argentina. Mount Aconcagua, the highest mountain peak in the Western Hemisphere, is located in Argentina.

ARGENTINA MAP EXERCISE

Refer to Map V on page 74 and locate the following cities with a dot and label them: Tucumán, Mendoza, Buenos Aires, and Córdoba. On the map, color the Chaco blue (1), the Pampas green (2), Patagonia yellow (3), and the Andes Mountains brown (4).

South America   Argentina: Reviewing What I Have Learned

Name _____   Date _____

REVIEWING WHAT I HAVE LEARNED

PHYSICAL FEATURES OF ARGENTINA

Complete the graphic organizer below by placing the names of the four main physical regions of Argentina in the rectangles.

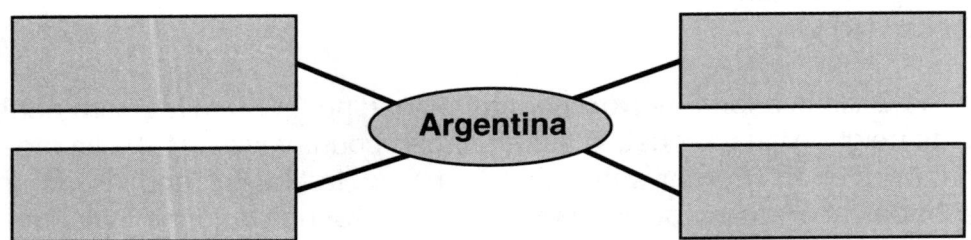

Match the definitions in Column B with the terms in column A. Place the letter of the definition on the line next to the corresponding term.

Column A
_____ 1. Mount Aconcagua
_____ 2. Chaco
_____ 3. Chile
_____ 4. Pampas
_____ 5. Lapacho
_____ 6. Andes
_____ 7. Patagonia
_____ 8. European
_____ 9. Quebracho
_____ 10. Buenos Aires

Column B
A. Argentina's western neighbor
B. Hard, beautiful wood used in buildings
C. High mountains on the western border
D. The capital of Argentina
E. Most of the population is of _____ extraction.
F. Tree known as the "axe breaker"
G. Subtropical region with forests of large trees
H. Fertile, grassy plain
I. Dry, windy plateau
J. Highest peak in the Western Hemisphere

BRAZIL

Area: 3,286,472 sq. miles
Population: 161,416,000; European 53%, Mulatto 22%, Mestizo 12%, African 4%, Japanese 1%, Amerindian 0.1%
Major Language: Portuguese
Major Religion: Roman Catholic
Independence: 1822

Brazil is the largest country in South America in square miles and in number of people. Brazil was settled by the **Portuguese**, so the major language spoken is Portuguese. Brazil became a Portuguese colony as a result of the **Treaty of Tordesillas** and the discovery of what is now Brazil by **Pedro Alvarez Cabral** in 1500. In 1822 Brazil was declared an independent empire, breaking away from Portugal. In 1889 Brazil became a republic. Over half of the people in Brazil are of European descent. Many of the people are **Mestizos**, which means they are mixed European and Native American. A small number of Indian tribes live in the Amazon Basin. Descendants of African natives brought as slaves to work the sugar plantations make up a small part of the population.

The **Coastal Lowlands** near the Atlantic Ocean produce large amounts of sugar cane, bananas, cotton, and cacao. The **Brazilian Highlands** inland from the coastal plain have large grassland areas with large numbers of cattle. The **Amazon Basin**, drained by the Amazon River, is where many large rubber plantations are found.

Most of the people of Brazil settled along the coast. The cities of Rio de Janeiro, Recife, Belém, and São Paulo are all located on or near the coast and have large populations. Inland cities include Belo Horizonte, Brasília, and Manaus on the Amazon River in the interior of Brazil.

Rio de Janeiro is located between the mountains and the sea with a beautiful beach. Rio is a city of over six million people. Rio has many beautiful buildings and beaches that are often crowded with people from all over the world who are vacationing. Visitors are welcomed by a huge statue of Christ on Mount Corcovado, which overlooks Rio de Janeiro. However, also on the mountainsides overlooking Rio, many poor people live in shacks. Many of these poor have moved from the interior of the country to Rio in hopes of finding work.

Belo Horizonte is the capital of the Brazilian state Minas Gerais. It is located away from the coast at an elevation of 2,600 feet above sea level. The climate is pleasant throughout the year. Belo Horizonte was a planned city built to look like Washington, D.C., in the United States. Belo Horizonte is a famous industrial city with steel mills. Brazilians love soccer, and one of the largest soccer stadiums in Brazil is located in Belo Horizonte. The city has many beautiful buildings, homes, and parks that have been designed by **Oscar Niemeyer**, a famous Brazilian architect.

Down the coast from Rio de Janeiro is **São Paulo**, the largest city in South America. São Paulo is the fastest growing city in Brazil with ten million people. This growth is a result of the business and employment opportunities in the city. People from all over Brazil come to the city in hopes of obtaining work. São Paulo is a city rich in cultures from various parts of the world, as well. In São Paulo one finds large numbers of Italians, Japanese, Arabs, and people from other parts of the world.

For much of its history, the city of Rio de Janeiro was the capital of Brazil. However, in 1960 the capital was moved to **Brasília**, a new city planned and developed by the government. Brasília is located 725 miles inland from Rio de Janeiro. It was hoped that by moving the capital inland it would encourage people to move from the coast and settle the interior of the country. Brasília is a very modern city with beautiful buildings. The plan for the city included wide beautiful streets and buildings laid out in the shape of an airplane. The plan was the work of Brazilian architects Costa and Niemeyer.

The city of **Recife** is known as the "Brazilian Venice." It has many canals, waterways, and bridges that connect the various parts of the city. The city has beautiful beaches protected from Atlantic storms by a barrier reef. Recife is an important cultural center with music and folklore festivals representing the many cultures that are found in the region. Like all Brazilian cities, there are beautiful churches and points of historical interest.

Belém is a famous coastal city located at the mouth of the Amazon River. The city is the main point of entry into the Amazon region. It became an important commercial and economic center based on rubber production. The marketplace in Belém is a center of activity as local products, crafts, fruits, and foods are brought in each morning by boat and canoe to be sold. The city also has many beautiful churches and historic buildings.

Many large sugar plantations are located along the northeastern coast of Brazil. In southern Brazil, in the state of Minas Gerais, is one of the most important farming regions where corn, soybeans, and cattle are raised.

The coffee plantations are also located in southern Brazil. Brazil is one of the world's leading coffee producers. The United States, Japan, and European countries buy large amounts of Brazilian coffee. Brazilians are fond of coffee and are often found in the cafeznios, drinking small cups of strong, black coffee known as **demitasse**.

Brazil also has large deposits of iron ore and petroleum. Belo Horizonte, located in southern Brazil, has become famous for steel production.

One of the major environmental problems facing Brazil is the destruction of the **Amazon rain forest** or **selvas**. The rain forest is a wet, hot region with many thunderstorms and temperatures that usually range from 70 to 85 degrees, but they can get much higher. A dense layer of trees form a canopy over the floor of the rain forest. Large areas of the rain forest are being cut for timber and in some areas for cattle grazing. The cutting of the rain forest is very destructive to the environment. The unprotected soils leach and soon become unproductive, habitat for animals and plants is destroyed, and the natives living in the rain forest must move deeper into the forest to survive. There are many who fear that the loss of the trees may affect the atmosphere as well, since the large amount of vegetation in the rain forest takes in carbon dioxide and gives off oxygen necessary for human survival.

BRAZIL MAP EXERCISE

1. On Map VI on page 75 color the following areas. Color the coastal plain (number 1) green, the Brazilian highlands grassland area (number 2) yellow, and the Amazon Basin area (number 3) blue. Use a blue pen to draw in the Amazon River and its tributaries.
2. Locate with a dot and label the following cities on Map VI: São Paulo, Rio de Janeiro, Brasília, Belém, Manaus, Recife, and Belo Horizonte.

South America   Brazil: Reviewing What I Have Learned

Name _____ Date _____

REVIEWING WHAT I HAVE LEARNED

Each statement below decribes one of the cities of Brazil. Read the descriptions and write the name of the city on the blank following each description.

1. This city is located inland. It is a planned city built to encourage the people of Brazil to move inland. The city was planned by two of Brazil's most famous architects, Costa and Niemeyer. The city is now the capital of Brazil. _____

2. This city is the largest city in South America. It is a fast-growing city with many people coming to the city to find work. _____

3. This city, located at the mouth of the Amazon River, became famous as a port where rubber was shipped to other parts of the world. It is the main point of entry into the Amazon region. Each morning, boats and canoes bring fruits, foods, and crafts to the market to be sold. _____

4. This city has beautiful beaches and is a vacation destination for people from all over the world. _____

5. This city has many canals, waterways, and bridges connecting various parts of the city. It is protected from Atlantic storms by a barrier reef. _____

6. This city was a planned city designed to look like Washington, D.C. It has become a major center for steel production. _____

Complete the table below listing the natural resources and agricultural products of Brazil.

Crops/Livestock	Natural Resources
_____	_____
_____	_____
_____	_____
_____	_____
_____	_____
_____	_____

© Mark Twain Media, Inc., Publishers

Venezuela

Area: 352,143 sq. miles
Population: 21,810,000; Mestizo 67%, European 21%, African 10%, Amerindian 2%
Major Religion: Roman Catholic
Major Language: Spanish
Independence: (From Spain) 1821; (Independent Republic) 1830

Venezuela is the northern-most country of South America. To the north of Venezuela lies the Caribbean Sea and to the east is the Atlantic Ocean. The **Andes Mountains**, **Lake Maracaibo**, the **Guiana Highlands**, and the **Orinoco River** basin are important physical features of Venezuela.

Maracaibo and **Caracas** are two important cities. Caracas, located in the Mérida Range of the Andes Mountains, is the capital. Located at this altitude, Caracas does not experience the hot, humid climate of a coastal location. Maracaibo, however, located near Lake Maracaibo, is hot and humid. It is an important port city.

The Orinoco River is one of the important rivers of South America. Each year, the land surrounding the Orinoco River goes through a very wet season and a very dry season. During the wet season, the river and surrounding area is often flooded. When the dry season comes, the floods subside and the region becomes very dry. Because of the alternating wet and dry seasons, the plains region around the Orinoco has large areas of grassland. This plains and grassland area is known as the **llanos**. It is an important cattle-raising area of Venezuela. The Orinoco is also an important transportation route for the iron mines found near the river. Iron ore mined up the river near El Pao is transported down the Orinoco to the Atlantic.

Venezuela is the leading oil-producing nation in South America. Rich deposits of oil are located near Lake Maracaibo. Most of the oil is shipped to the United States. The production and export of oil has made it possible for Venezuela to have one of the highest standards of living in South America. However, the government realizes that the oil reserves will be depleted early in the next century. To maintain the standard of living, the government is encouraging the development of other industries so the nation will be less dependent on oil. One effort by the government has been to encourage the development of more productive farming on the plains of the llanos.

Venezuela is also the birthplace of **Simón Bolívar**, whom many have called the "George Washington of South America." Bolívar was a **Creole** who believed that the countries of South America should become independent. Early in the history of South America, those who had immigrated from Spain had a higher social standing than those who were born of Spanish parents on South American soil. *Creole* was the term used for such a person. Since Bolívar was born in Venezuela of Spanish parents, he was a Creole. Bolívar had read about the United States gaining independence from Great Britain by winning the Revolutionary War. He believed that South American countries could become independent like the United States.

In 1821 Venezuela gained independence from Spain and joined the republic of **Gran Colombia**, which included Colombia, Venezuela, Ecuador, and Panama. In 1830 Venezuela broke away from Gran Colombia to become an independent republic.

South America · Venezuela: Reviewing What I Have Learned

Name _____ Date _____

Venuzuela Map Exercise

Refer to Map VII on page 76 and locate and label the following. Draw in the river and place dots for the cities.

Caribbean Sea **Atlantic Ocean** **Lake Maracaibo** **El Pao**
Orinoco River **Caracas**   **Maracaibo**

Write the term "Llanos" along the line labeled "a - - - b" on the map of Venezuela.

Reviewing What I Have Learned

Match the definition in Column B with the correct term in Column A. Place the letter of the correct definition next to the corresponding term.

Column A

_____ 1. Llanos
_____ 2. Maracaibo
_____ 3. Caracas
_____ 4. Orinoco
_____ 5. El Pao
_____ 6. Bolívar
_____ 7. Creole
_____ 8. Caribbean
_____ 9. Cattle
_____ 10. Oil

Column B

A. River in Venezuela
B. Sea on north coast of Venezuela
C. Iron ore mine in Venezuela
D. Oil-exporting city located on Lake Maracaibo
E. Venezuela's most important natural resource
F. Capital city of Venezuela located in the highlands
G. Grassland plains near Orinoco River
H. Led the movement for independence from Spain
I. Refers to a European born in South America
J. Product grown on the Llanos

© Mark Twain Media, Inc., Publishers

Colombia

Area: 439,733 sq. miles
Population: 34,948,000; Mestizo 58%, European 20%, Mulatto 14%, African 4%,
Mixed African and Indian 3%, Amerindian 1%
Major Religion: Roman Catholic
Major Language: Spanish
Independence: 1819

In Colombia the **Magdalena** and **Cauca Rivers** are important physical features. They are important because these rivers flow down mountain valleys that split the Andes into three branches. It is in these mountain valleys that most of the people of Colombia live. The cities of Bogotá, Cali, and Medellín are located in the valleys formed by these rivers. The rivers flow eastward out of the high Andes until they reach the Caribbean Sea. Along the coast of the Caribbean are the coastal cities of Cartagena and Barranquilla.

It is in the highland valleys that one of Colombia's most important crops is raised. The crop is coffee. It is raised on the mountainsides. In these highlands many farmers also raise small grains and potatoes. In the lowlands where the climate is more hot and humid, crops like bananas, sugar cane, and cotton are raised.

When the Spanish conquistadors came to Colombia, they were looking for gold. The myth of **El Dorado** encouraged the Spanish explorers to believe they would find large amounts of gold in Colombia. According to the myth, there existed an Indian king who covered himself with gold dust every day and washed it off in a pool once each year. Although the Spanish never found El Dorado, they did find gold. The gold was shipped back to Spain, and it encouraged the Spaniards to continue searching for the precious metal. They finally found huge quantities of gold in the Incan Empire in Ecuador, Peru, Bolivia, and Chile. After conquering the Incas, the Spanish shipped millions of dollars worth of precious metal back to Spain.

Today, Colombia produces gold and other precious minerals like emeralds. Colombia is one of the world's major producers of emeralds. Coal, oil, and iron ore are also found in Columbia.

Colombia Map Exercise

Refer to Map VII on page 76 and complete the following.

1. Along line "a - - - b" on the map of Colombia, draw the symbols "www" to indicate the western chain of the Andes.
2. Along line "c - - - d", draw the symbols "ccc" to indicate the central chain of the Andes.
3. Along line "e - - - f", draw the symbols "eee" to indicate the eastern chain of the Andes.
4. Locate the following cities by placing a dot on the map and writing the name of the city by the dot: **Bogotá, Medellín, Cali, Barranquilla, Cartagena.**
5. Draw in the rivers with a blue pen or pencil and label the following bodies of water: **Pacific Ocean, Caribbean Sea, Cauca River, Magdalena River.**

South America

Colombia: Reviewing What I Have Learned

Name _____ Date _____

Reviewing What I Have Learned

Fill in the top rectangle and the four smaller rectangles in the graphic organizer below using the following terms. Use the number of blanks below each rectangle as a clue to help you title each rectangle.

Crops   **Colombia**   **Port Cities**   **Highland Cities**   **Natural Resources**

Complete the blanks below each rectangle using the following terms.

Bogotá	bananas	sugar cane	**Medellín**	emeralds
coal	**Cali**	iron ore	gold	**Barranquilla**
Cartagena	oil	coffee	cotton	

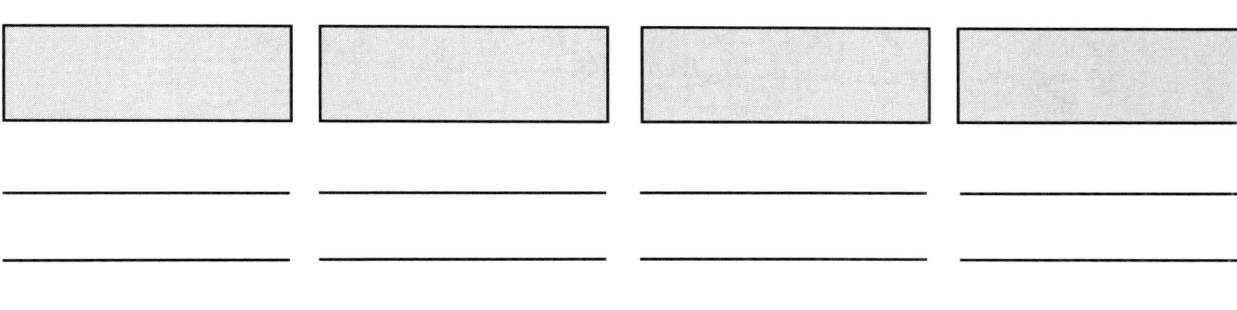

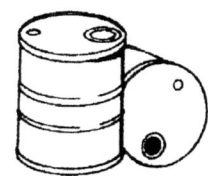

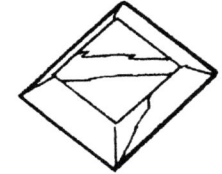

© Mark Twain Media, Inc., Publishers   41

Peru, Ecuador, and Bolivia

Peru, Ecuador, and Bolivia are all countries located in the high Andes. All three countries have a population that includes large numbers of Indians who are descendants of the Indians of the Inca Empire. Mestizos, those with mixed European and Indian ancestry, are the second most numerous population group.

These countries all have plateau areas located in the high Andes at elevations of 10,000 feet or more. In all three countries, the Andes form two very high chains of mountains. It is between these chains on high plateaus that large numbers of people live and work. In Bolivia the high plain is known as the Altiplano. Bolivia is landlocked, but Ecuador and Peru extend westward to the Pacific Ocean. Peru and Ecuador both have very important port cities located on the Pacific Ocean, as well as cities located in the highlands.

Peru, Ecuador, and Bolivia Map Exercise

Use an atlas and refer to Map VIII on page 77. Locate the following cities by placing a dot where the city is located. Write the name of the city by the dot.

Guayaquil	**Quito**	**Calloa**	**Lima**
La Paz	**Sucre**	**Iquitos**	**Cuzco**

South America   Ecuador

Name _____ Date _____

ECUADOR

Area: 109,483 sq. miles
Population: 11,384,000; Mestizo 40%, Amerindian 40%, European 15%, African 5%
Major Religion: Roman Catholic
Major Language: Spanish
Independence: (From Spain) 1822; (Independent Republic) 1830

Ecuador has three outstanding physical features. The **Pacific coastal plain**, the **high Andes**, and the **lowlands of eastern Ecuador**. Most of the people live in the **fertile basins** (marked "C" in the diagram below) located between the eastern and western ranges of the Andes. The diagram below is a profile of Ecuador, from the coastal plain in the west to the tropical lowlands in the east.

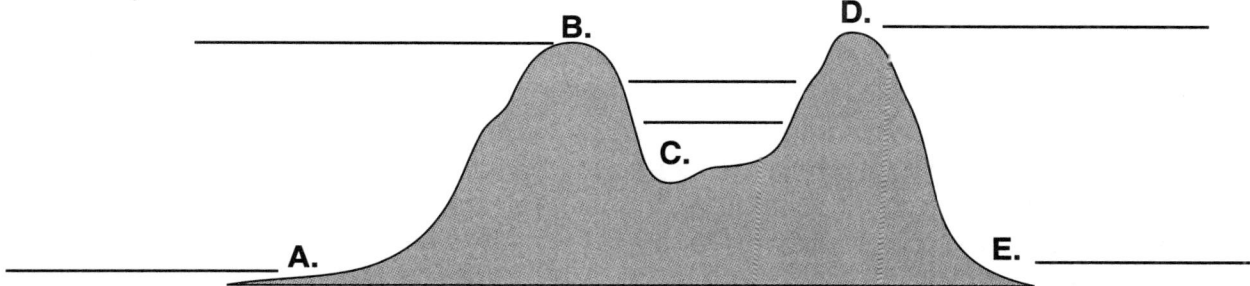

Write each of the following terms on the blanks above the correct location on the profile.

Western Andes   **Eastern Andes**   **Pacific Coastal Plain**
Tropical Lowlands   **Mountain Basins**

The Pacific coastal plain in the north is very wet and hot. The southern part of the coastal plain is dry, with desert-like conditions in many places.
The **Galapagos Islands** in the Pacific Ocean also belong to Ecuador. Scientists, such as Charles Darwin, have studied the unusual plant and animal life found there.
Crops like cacao, coffee, and bananas are grown for export in Ecuador. Farmers living on the high plateau raise subsistence crops like corn, beans, potatoes, and small grain crops. The eastern lowlands is a tropical region that was unimportant until the discovery of oil, which is now one of Ecuador's major exports.
The land that makes up present-day Ecuador was once part of the **Inca Empire**. The influences of the Indian empire and the Spanish conquistadors are reflected in today's population. While there is a large Indian population, an almost equal number of the people are of mixed European and Indian descent (**Mestizo**).

ECUADOR MAP EXERCISE

Refer to Map VIII on page 77. The area marked "a" on the map is the wet and hot coastal plain area of Ecuador, the area marked "b" is the dry and hot coastal plain area, the area marked "c" is the high plateau area, and the area marked "d" is the tropical lowland area. Color each area a different color.

Peru

Area: 496,223 sq. miles
Population: 23,588,000; Quechua 47%, Mestizo 32%, European 12%, Aymara 5%
Major Religion: Roman Catholic
Major Language: Spanish and Quechua (both official)
Independence: 1821

In Peru, native Indians are a large part of the population. Many of these Indians are descendants of the natives who were part of the great **Inca Empire**. **Cuzco** was the capital of the Inca Empire, and **Machu Picchu** is the site of major ruins left by the ancient civilization. Large numbers of Indians still live in mountain villages, raising potatoes, beans, and corn. Like Ecuador and Bolivia, the population of Peru also includes many Mestizos.

The **Pacific coastal plain** of Peru is dry and desert-like. Where streams from the mountains flow across the coastal plain to the ocean, some areas are irrigated and are highly productive. Crops raised on these irrigated areas of the coastal plain include cotton, sugar cane, and rice. These crops are raised on commercial farms and are exported to other countries of the world. However, except for the irrigated areas, most of the coastal plain is uninhabited. The **high plateau** areas between the eastern and western branches of the Andes are areas of subsistence farming. Farmers raise corn, beans, potatoes, and small grain crops in the cool climate. Once the Andes are crossed, one descends into the hot, wet, **tropical region** in eastern Peru. It is in this eastern area that important oil deposits have been found. Oil exports make up a significant part of the export income of Peru.

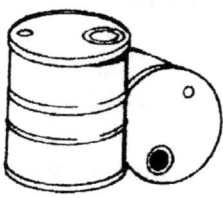   

Peru Map Exercise

Draw in the borders for the following regions and color each with the color indicated.
1. Pacific coastal plain: yellow
2. High plateau: brown
3. Tropical region: green

South America   Peru

Name _____ Date _____

PERU (CONTINUED)

Match each definition in Column B with the correct term in Column A.

Column A   **Column B**

_____ 1. Productive   A. Products produced and sold to other countries
_____ 2. Subsistence   B. Means that people do not live there
_____ 3. Uninhabited   C. Regions near the equator that are usually hot and wet
_____ 4. Descend   D. Refers to fertile areas where crops are raised
_____ 5. Tropical   E. Producing only enough for one's own family
_____ 6. Exports   F. Means to move from a higher to a lower region
_____ 7. Commercial   G. Refers to farms that produce goods to be sold for profit

Refer to the selection on Peru and complete the following chart by placing the following terms beneath the correct main headings. Place those terms in #1 first. Some of the terms in #2 may be used under more than one of the major headings.

1. subsistence farming, oil production, commercial farming
2. beans, oil, potatoes, cotton, rice, sugar cane, grains, corn, hot, cool, wet, dry

Pacific Coastal Area	High Plateaus	Eastern Tropical Area
_____	_____	_____
_____	_____	_____
_____	_____	_____
_____	_____	_____
_____	_____	_____
_____	_____	_____

Bolivia

Area: 424,162 sq. miles
Population: 7,900,000; Mestizo 31%, Quechua 25%, Aymara 17%, European 15%
Major Religion: Roman Catholic
Major Languages: Spanish, Quechua, Aymara (all official)
Independence: 1825

Bolivia is one of two landlocked countries in South America. A high plateau called the **Altiplano** is the most important area of Bolivia. Most of the people live here. The high Altiplano lies at an elevation of 12,000 feet between the eastern and western Andes. The high peaks of the eastern and western Andes rise to altitudes of over 20,000 feet and look down on the Altiplano below.

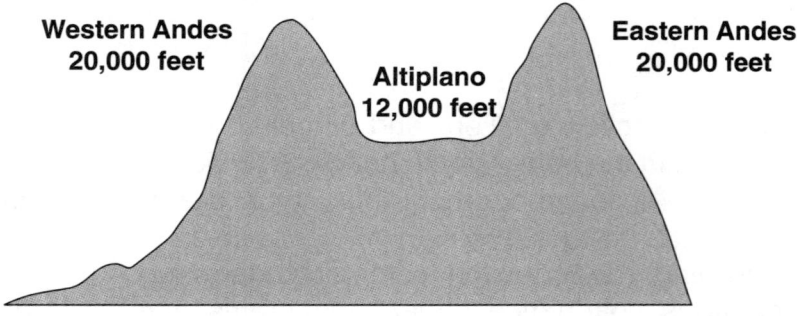

The Altiplano is a high plateau that includes many valleys. Since the elevation is 12,000 feet, the days and nights are often chilly. However, crops like potatoes, small grains like rye, and beans can be raised. These crops form the main diet of the people. The population living on the Altiplano is mostly engaged in subsistence agriculture.

The Altiplano was very important during the Inca Empire. Here in the valleys on this high plateau, the Inca civilization prospered. Today, the large Indian population of the Altiplano still practices many of the cultural habits of the Incas.

Two of the most impressive physical features of the Altiplano are **Lake Titicaca** and **Lake Poopó**. These lakes are an important part of the lives of the Indians who live on the Altiplano. The lakes make the climate of the surrounding area a few degrees warmer than would be expected at this high altitude. The result is that small grain crops like rye can mature at an altitude that would not be possible if the lakes were not present. The lakes also furnish water to the region. The importance of the lakes was recognized and used by the Incas to grow crops and maintain an advanced society at this high altitude.

Since Bolivia is a landlocked country, influences from the outside world are not as prevalent as in other South American countries. Nearly 85 percent of the population is either native Indian or Mestizo. Many are descendants of the Incas. The influences of the Incas are still evident today as one looks at the life styles of the Indians who inhabit most of the Altiplano. About 15 percent of the population is of European descent.

The most important exports of Bolivia are tin, tungsten, silver, and gold; although, in recent years, oil has been found and produces some export income.

La Paz is the administrative capital and Sucre is the legal capital of Bolivia. Also located high in the Altiplano are the ruins of cities of the Inca civilization.

South America   Bolivia

Name _____ Date _____

BOLIVIA (CONTINUED)

Use the terms below and complete the blanks in the following selection.

Altiplano	**potatoes**	**La Paz**	**beans**	**Mestizos**
oil	**Sucre**	**rye**	**tin**	**Titicaca**
European	**silver**	**Indians**	**warmer**	**subsistence**

    In Bolivia most of the population live on the high (1) _____. Here they are (2) _____ farmers, raising crops like (3) _____, (4) _____, and (5) _____.

    A large lake on the Altiplano is Lake (6) _____. The large lakes of Bolivia make the Altiplano a few degrees (7) _____ than it would be otherwise.

    The most important exports of Bolivia are (8) _____, tungsten, (9) _____ , and gold. Recently, exports of (10) _____ have added to the income of Bolivia.

    The capital cities are (11) _____ and (12) _____ .

    The majority of the population are (13)_____ or (14) _____ . Only about 15 percent of the population are of (15) _____ descent.

BOLIVIA MAP EXERCISE

Refer to Map VIII on page 78 and complete the following.

1. Draw in Lake Titicaca and Lake Poopó.

2. If you have not already done so on this map, locate and label La Paz and Sucre.

3. On the map, write the names of the countries along the borders they share with Bolivia.

South America — Peru, Ecuador, and Bolivia: Reviewing What I Have Learned

Name _____ Date _____

REVIEWING WHAT I HAVE LEARNED

Use the following cities, countries, and physical features to complete the blanks in the selection below.

Cities: Guayaquil, Quito, Callao, Lima, Cuzco, La Paz, Sucre, Iquitos
Countries: Peru, Bolivia, Ecuador, Brazil, Colombia, Chile, Paraguay
Physical Features: Mt. Chimborazo, Lake Titicaca, Amazon River, Mt. Cotopax

This capital city is located in the high Andes near the equator. Although it is only one-half degree from the equator, it is neither hot nor rainy. Its location high in the Andes makes the nights in this city very chilly and the days cool. In the distance, the snow-covered peaks of (1) _____ and (2) _____ can be seen. This city is (3) _____. A short distance away on the Pacific coast is a busy port city. This city is at a much lower elevation, so the days and nights are much warmer. This port city is (4) _____. The country is (5) _____. Its Spanish-speaking neighbors are the countries of (6) _____ and (7) _____.

Located on the Altiplano south of Lake Titicaca is the city (8) _____. It is one of the two capital cities of (9) _____. Located still farther south is the other capital city, (10) _____. To the south are the Spanish-speaking countries (11) _____, (12) _____, and (13) _____. On the eastern border is the largest country in South America. The people in this country speak Portuguese. This Portuguese-speaking country is (14) _____.

Many ancient ruins from the Inca Empire are located in this country. Lake Titicaca on the Altiplano is shared with Bolivia. This country has a long coastal lowland near the Pacific Ocean. It also has a high Andes region and a large area extending into the Amazon Basin. This country is (15) _____. An important city is the port city of (16) _____. Only a few miles from this port city, but located in the highlands, is the capital city (17) _____. In the high Andes, just north of Lake Titicaca, is a city that was the capital of the Inca Empire. This city is (18) _____. Another important port city of this country is located in the eastern lowlands of the Amazon Basin. From this port city goods move down the (19) _____ to the Atlantic Ocean. This city is (20) _____.

Chile

Area: 292,258 sq. miles
Population: 14,271,000; Mestizo 92%, Amerindian 6%, European 2%
Major Religion: Roman Catholic
Major Language: Spanish
Independence: 1818

Chile is a unique country. It extends over 2,600 miles from its northern border, with Peru to the southern tip of South America. Although Chile is a long country, it is very narrow. The greatest distance from the Pacific Ocean to the eastern boundary of the country is only about 260 miles.

The climates of Chile include the **desert climate** found in the Atacama Desert in northern Chile, the **Mediterranean climate** of central Chile, and the **mid-latitude marine climate** in southern Chile. The Atacama Desert in most years is one of the driest deserts in the world. However, in years when the El Niño current occurs, this normally dry area can become very wet. The central part of Chile with the Mediterranean climate has long, warm summers and mild, wet winters. In the south, the mid-latitude climate has cool, moist summers and chilly, wet winters.

The Central Valley of Chile is the productive central valley area. Crops like wheat, grapes, and fruits are grown here. Many farms are devoted to the raising of cattle and sheep. This is one of the most important agricultural areas in South America. Many of the crops raised here are exported to other parts of the world.

In the far south of Chile, one of the most prominent features is the snow-capped Andes. Snow-capped mountains, glaciers moving down valleys toward the sea, and icebergs remind one of northern Norway.

Chile is one of the world's largest producers of copper. The Atacama Desert is an important copper-producing area.

The history of Chile has been different than the other South American countries. When other parts of South America were brought under the control of the Spanish, Chile remained an outpost area garrisoned with an army. For many years, the army could not secure the country because of the resistance of the fierce Araucanian Indians. The Araucanian Indians retreated into the southern part of Chile, making it very difficult for the Spanish to defeat them. Eventually, the army overcame the Araucanians, and Chile began its journey to the present.

Santiago is the capital of Chile and is located in the Central Valley. Valparaíso, a short distance from Santiago, is a port city on the Pacific. Farther south, the city of Concepción is an important city.

More than 90 percent of the people of Chile are Mestizos. Pure Indians are only a small part of the population. The remainder of the population is primarily Europeans with Swiss, Italian, or German heritage.

South America   Chile

Name _____ Date _____

CHILE (CONTINUED)

CHILE MAP EXERCISE

Refer to Map V on page 74 and complete the following.

1. Place a dot on the map to locate the following cities: Santiago, Concepción, Antofagasta, and Valparaíso.
2. Place the symbol "***" on the map to locate the Atacama Desert.
3. Place the symbol "AAA" to locate the Andes Mountains.
4. Place the symbol "+" to locate Mt. Aconcagua.
5. Locate Cape Horn by writing the name at the location.

Complete the following chart. Write the terms below beneath the correct heading in the chart.

Atacama Desert	**grapes**	**glaciers**	**agricultural area**
chilly, wet winters	**wheat**	**fruits**	**very dry**
copper	**cool summers**	**warm summers**	**mild, moist winters**
cattle	**Santiago**	**Concepción**	**Antofagasta**
Valparaíso			

Northern Chile	Central Chile	Southern Chile
_____	_____	_____
_____	_____	_____
_____	_____	_____
_____	_____	_____
_____	_____	_____
_____	_____	_____
_____	_____	_____
_____	_____	_____
_____	_____	_____

South America   Chile: Reviewing What I Have Learned

Name _____ Date _____

REVIEWING WHAT I HAVE LEARNED

Use the terms below and complete the blanks in the following selection.

Cape Horn	**Bolivia**	2,600	mestizo	**El Niño**
Atacama	**Peru**	260	Italy	**Central Valley**

In the north, Chile borders the nations of (1) _____ and (2) _____. The distance from the northern border with Peru to the southern boundary at (3) _____ is a distance over (4) _____ miles. Although a long country, it is very narrow, being only (5) _____ miles from west to east. The most productive area is found in the (6) _____, where cattle, wheat, grapes, and other fruits are raised.

In the northern region, one of the driest deserts in the world is the (7) _____. Although usually very dry, in years when the (8) _____ current occurs, this desert region becomes very wet.

The population of Chile is mostly (9) _____. The European population includes people from Switzerland, Germany, and (10) _____.

Complete the following chart.

1. Write the term **Mestizo** under nations where Mestizos are the major population group.
2. Write the term **Indian** under nations where Indians are the major population group.
3. Write the term **landlocked** under nations that are landlocked.
4. Write the term **desert** under nations with desert areas.
5. Write the term **Andes** under nations with mountain areas.
6. Write the term **Spanish** under nations where Spanish is spoken.
7. Write the term **equator** under nations that lie on the equator.
8. Write the term **Altiplano** under nations where the plateau is located.
9. Write the term **copper** under nations that are major producers.
10. Write the term **oil** under nations that are major producers.

Ecuador	**Peru**	**Bolivia**	**Chile**

© Mark Twain Media, Inc., Publishers

Paraguay

Area: 157,046 sq. miles
Population: 4,979,000; Mestizo 90%, Amerindian 3%
Major Religion: Roman Catholic
Major Languages: Spanish, Guaraní (both official)
Independence: 1811

Paraguay gained its independence from Spain in 1811. For most of its history, the nation has remained isolated and ruled by dictators. Today Paraguay, like the rest of South America, is moving toward a democratic government. One of the most disastrous events was the Paraguan War with Brazil, Argentina, and Uruguay, which lasted from 1865 to 1870. In the end, Paraguay was defeated, and more than half of the population lost their lives.

Eastern Paraguay has a humid, subtropical climate with forests and grasslands. The western part of Paraguay is the Chaco region. The Chaco has wet summers and dry winters. In the western part of the Chaco, the famous, huge trees, like the quebracha, are found. This tree has extremely hard wood. Its bark and wood contain tannin, which is used to tan leather. Yerba Mate is a green tea made from the bark of the Yerba tree, also found in this region. The Chaco also includes large areas of grassland. In the east, near Brazil, the Chaco becomes drier and its grass becomes very sparse.

Paraguay is one of the landlocked countries of South America. Paraguay is about the same size as California. Even though it is landlocked, the Paraguay and Paraná rivers provide a transportation route to the Atlantic. Paraguay ships most of its goods down the Paraná, to the Rio de la Plata at Buenos Aires, Argentina.

Asunción is the capital and largest city. It is located on the Paraguay River, and across the river is Argentina. Asunción is the largest city in Paraguay. There are few natural resources. Most of the people are engaged in farming. Although many are subsistence farmers, there is a large production of cattle and cotton.

Most of the people live east of the Paraguay River. Mestizos make up most of the population. Spanish and Guaraní are the two official languages spoken in Paraguay. Guaraní is an Indian language spoken by the Indians who lived in the area when the Spaniards arrived.

In an effort to become a more modern nation, Paraguay has cooperated with Brazil to build a large, hydroelectric plant on the Paraná River. Brazil and Paraguay cooperatively built the Itaipú Dam, the world's largest dam. The dam creates a reservoir of water that when released turns the turbines and produces electricity. Paraguay sells a large part of the electrical power produced to Brazil.

South America   Paraguay

Name _____ Date _____

Paraguay (Continued)

Paraguay Map Exercise

Use Map IX on page 78 and complete the following activities.

1. Write the names of the countries on the map that border Paraguay.
2. Locate the Chaco region in Paraguay by using the letters (cccccc).
3. Place a dot to locate the capital city and write the name of the capital by the dot.
4. Use a blue pencil and draw in the Paraná River on the map.
5. Color that part of Paraguay located in the tropics red.
6. Place a symbol on the map to show where the large dam built by Paraguay and Brazil is located. Write "hydroelectric power" by the symbol.

The table below shows the average monthly temperatures and rainfall amounts in inches for a city in eastern Paraguay. Refer to the table and answer the questions below.

	JAN	FEB	MAR	APR	MAY	JUN	JUL	AUG	SEP	OCT	NOV	DEC
Temperature:	81	80	78	72	67	63	64	66	70	73	76	80
Rainfall (inches):	5.5	5.1	4.3	5.2	4.6	2.7	2.2	1.6	3.1	5.5	5.9	6.2

1. The three months with the warmest temperatures are: _____

2. The three months with the coolest temperatures are: _____

3. Summer occurs in all or part of the following months in Paraguay: _____

4. Winter occurs in all or part of the following months in Paraguay: _____

5. Winter temperatures in Paraguay are warm, because much of Paraguay is located:

   (a) in the tropics (b) in the highlands (c) near the ocean.

6. The four months with the most rainfall are: _____

7. The three months with the least rainfall are: _____

South America　　　　　　　　　　　　　　Paraguay: Reviewing What I Have Learned

Name _____ Date _____

REVIEWING WHAT I HAVE LEARNED

Complete the blanks in each of the following sentences. Select your answers from the words listed below.

Chaco	**Spanish**	**Paraná**	**landlocked**
Mestizos	**quebracho**	**Guaraní**	**hydroelectric**
subsistence	**Yerba Mate**	**Brazil**	**Paraguay**

1. The languages spoken in Paraguay are (a) _____ and (b) _____.
2. Most of the population of Paraguay are mixed European and Indians known as _____.
3. The major rivers of Paraguay are the _____ and the _____.
4. The famous tea in Paraguay made from the bark of the yerba tree is known as _____.
5. Paraguay is entirely surrounded by other nations. Since Paraguay does not have any part of its borders facing the ocean, it is a _____ country.
6. In Paraguay, a tree grows with extremely hard wood. The bark and wood of the tree contain tannin. The tree is the _____ tree.
7. Farmers in Paraguay who raise only enough food for their own use are _____ farmers.
8. Paraguay and _____ cooperated to build a large dam on the Paraná.
9. The dam was built to produce _____ power.
10. When the Spanish arrived in the part of South America that is now Paraguay, the Indians living in the area were the _____.

Name _____ Date _____

PARAGUAY CROSSWORD PUZZLE

Use the clues below to complete the crossword puzzle about Paraguay. Answers may be found in the information about Paraguay on page 52.

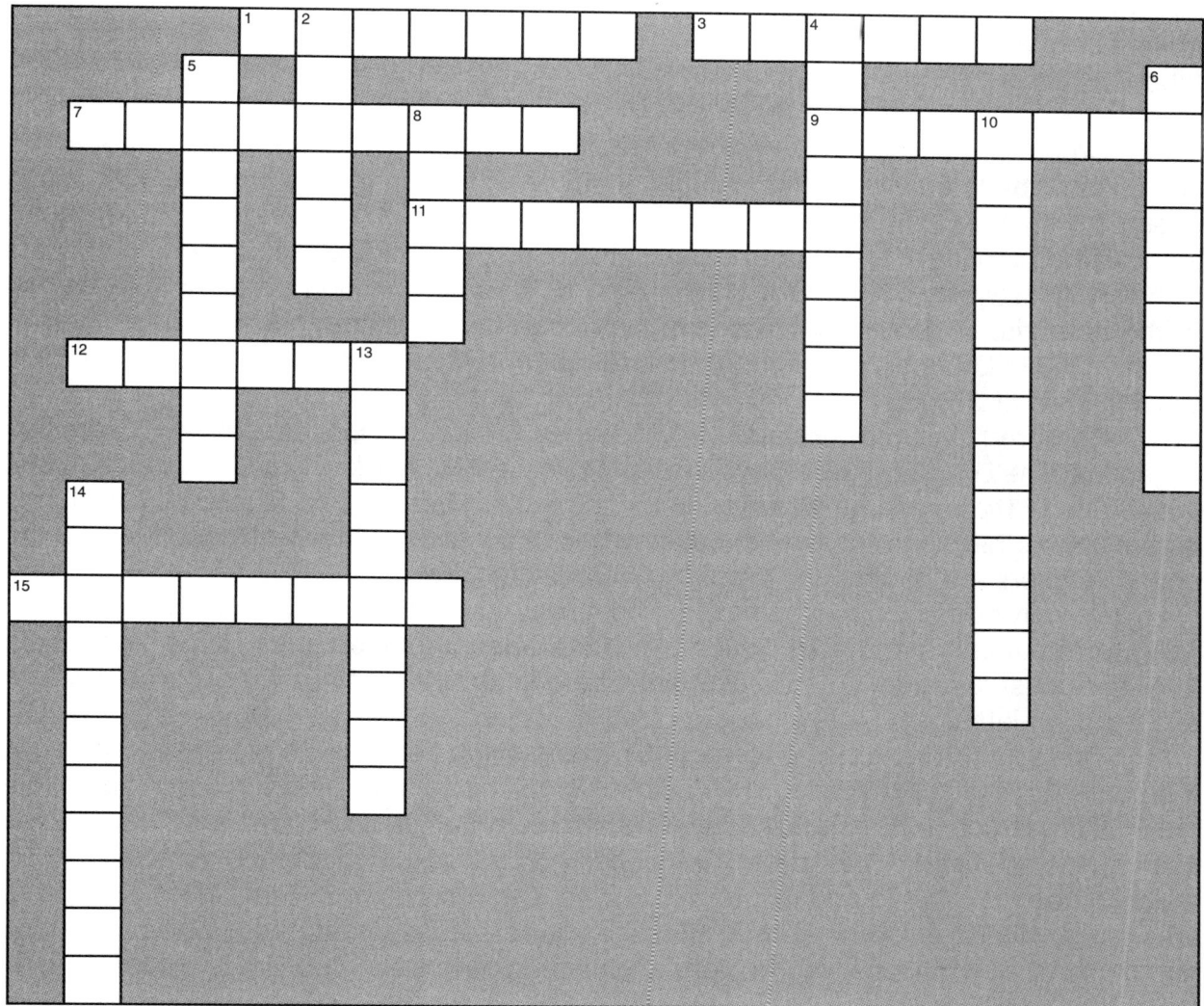

ACROSS
1. One of the official languages spoken in Paraguay
3. The name of the dam on the Paraná River
7. A tree with very hard wood
9. The native people who inhabited Paraguay when the Spanish arrived
11. The capital of Paraguay
12. The country that cooperated with Paraguay to build a dam on the Paraná River
15. People of mixed Spanish and Indian descent

DOWN
2. A major river that forms the southeastern border of Paraguay
4. Paraguay's neighbor to the south
5. The tea drunk in Paraguay (two words)
6. For most of its history, Paraguay was ruled by _____.
8. An area of forest and grassland in western Paraguay
10. The major religion of Paraguay
13. With no border facing an ocean, Paraguay is a _____ country.
14. The major port to which goods from Paraguay are shipped (two words)

Uruguay

Area: 68,498 sq. miles
Population: 3,186,000; European 86%, Mestizo 8%, Mulatto or African 6%
Major Religions: Roman Catholic 66%, Protestant 2%, Judaism 1%
Major Language: Spanish
Independence: 1828

Uruguay was first discovered by a Spanish navigator in 1516, but it was very sparsely settled until the late seventeenth century. In an effort to stop the Portuguese from taking over the area, the Spanish founded Montevideo, the capital of Uruguay, in 1726. Uruguay, along with Argentina, Paraguay, and parts of Bolivia, Brazil, and Chile, became part of the Spanish **Viceroyalty of La Plata**. However, in 1820 Brazil annexed Uruguay. Like the rest of the countries in South America, Uruguay soon began a struggle for independence. Finally, in 1828 Uruguay was recognized by Brazil and Argentina as the independent Eastern Republic of Uruguay.

Bordered by bodies of water on three sides, Uruguay is located between Brazil and Argentina. The Uruguay River forms the country's western border. The Atlantic Ocean and the Rio de la Plata, a large **estuary**, form its southern border. The Cuareim River forms part of the northern border, and the major river of the interior is the Rio Negro. Many of the country's rivers are dammed to produce hydroelectric power.

Largely due to its location near the ocean, Uruguay has a mild climate with comfortably warm summers and mild winters. Average annual temperatures range from about 50°F in August to around 75°F in January. There is a **rainy season** in April and May with average annual rainfall of 35 inches.

The country is a grass-covered plain in the south rising to a high, sandy plateau in the north. Agricultural products, such as beef, wool, hides, and leather goods, make up a majority of the country's exports. There are also commercial tree plantations where trees such as the quebracho are grown. The wood and bark of the quebracho contains tannin, which is used in tanning and dyeing processes. Other crops grown include maize, potatoes, sugar beets, and wheat. Industries include textiles, cement, tires, food processing and packing, hydroelectric power, light engineering, and steel. Tourism is also an important industry in Uruguay.

Uruguay Map Exercise

Refer to Map IX on page 78 and locate and label the following bodies of water and cities on the map. Draw in the rivers with a blue pen or colored pencil, and place a dot where the cities should be located.

Rio de la Plata	**Rio Negro**	**Uruguay River**	**Rio Negro Reservoir**
Atlantic Ocean	**Lake Mirim**	**Montevideo**	**Salto**

Reviewing What I Have Learned

Use the following terms to fill in the blanks in the selection about Uruguay.

Viceroyalty **Rio Negro** estuary **Argentina**
Portuguese **Brazil** rainy **Montevideo**
water **seventeenth**

Few Europeans settled in Uruguay until the late (1) _____ century. To prevent Uruguay's neighbors, the (2) _____ from taking over the area, the Spanish founded the capital of Uruguay, (3) _____. Uruguay then became part of the Spanish (4) _____ of La Plata. In 1828 Uruguay's independence was recognized by (5) _____ and (6) _____.

Uruguay is bordered by (7) _____ on three sides. The Atlantic Ocean and the Rio de la Plata, a large (8) _____ form the southern border. The major river of the interior is the (9) _____.

Uruguay has mild seasonal temperatures with a (10) _____ season in April and May.

Complete the table below by filling in the agricultural products and the industries of Uruguay.

Agriculture	Industry
_____	_____
_____	_____
_____	_____
_____	_____
_____	_____
_____	_____
_____	_____
_____	_____

SURINAM, GUYANA, AND FRENCH GUIANA

You have learned that the Spanish and Portuguese were the two European nations that explored and settled large parts of South America. However, there were three small countries in South America settled by the Dutch, British, and French. These countries are Surinam, Guyana, and French Guiana. During the colonial period, many African slaves were also brought to this part of South America to work on the plantations.

SURINAM

Area: 63,039 sq. miles
Population: 421,000; Asian Indian 37%, Creole (mixed White and Black) 31%, Indonesian 14%, African 9%, Amerindian 3%, Chinese 3%, Dutch 1%
Major Religions: Hinduism 27%, Christianity (Roman Catholic 23%, Protestant 19%), Islam 20%
Major Language: Dutch
Independence: 1975

Surinam is a country that was originally settled by the English in 1651 and then was given to the Netherlands in 1667 in exchange for the New Amsterdam colony in North America. For many years it was known as Dutch Guiana. African slaves were brought in to work the plantations that produced cocoa, coffee, cotton, and sugar. When slavery was abolished in 1863, workers from India and Indonesia were brought in to work the plantations. In 1975, this nation gained its independence from the Netherlands. The language spoken here is Dutch. The main exports of Surinam are bauxite and aluminum. Bauxite is the natural resource from which aluminum is refined. Other exports include shrimp, rice, bananas, and timber.

GUYANA

Area: 83,000 sq. miles
Population: 832,000; Asian Indian 49%, African 36%, Mulatto 7%, Amerindian 7%, Portuguese, Chinese
Major Religions: Christianity (Protestant 34%, Roman Catholic 18%), Hinduism 34%, Islam 9%
Major Language: English
Independence: 1966

Although originally settled by the Dutch in 1581, Guyana became a colony of the British known as British Guiana in 1831. When slavery was abolished in 1838, Asian laborers were brought in to replace the African slaves. British Guiana became independent in 1966, and it was renamed Guyana. English is the language spoken in Guyana. Plantation agriculture is important in Guyana. Rice, sugar cane, and citrus fruits are raised and exported.

FRENCH GUIANA

Area: 34,749 sq. miles
Population: 154,000; Creole 42%, Chinese 14%, French 10%, Haitian 7%
Major Religion: Roman Catholic
Major Language: French
Not Independent: French Protectorate

French Guiana is still a protectorate of France, having been first settled by the French in 1604. The economy depended on plantation farming, so African slaves were brought in to work the plantations. After slavery was abolished in 1848, Asian laborers were brought in to take the place of the slaves. French Guiana was used as a settlement for political prisoners by the French from the time of the French Revolution in the 1790s. There are no major exports from French Guiana. It depends on France for money, but it has earned some money for France at the European Space Agency's rocket-launching facility in Kourou. Agriculture is mosty subsistence farming, with rice being the main crop. The language spoken is French.

SURINAM, GUYANA, AND FRENCH GUIANA MAP EXERCISE

Refer to Map VII on page 76 and complete the following activities.

1. Locate Surinam, Guyana, and French Guiana. Write the names of the countries on the map.

2. Place a dot to locate the capital cities: Georgetown, Paramaribo, and Cayenne. Write the name of the city next to the dot.

South America

Name _____ Date _____

REVIEWING WHAT I HAVE LEARNED

Complete the following chart to show the influence of European nations on the culture of South America. Do not place anything on blanks with an "X". Use the following terms for the columns titled "Religion" and "Language." The first one has been completed for you.

Catholic Spanish Portuguese English Dutch French
Spanish/Quechua   Spanish/Quechua/Aymara   Spanish/Guaraní

Country	Major Religion	Language(s)	Population
1. Venezuela	Catholic	Spanish	21,810,000
2. Colombia			
3. Ecuador			
4. Peru			
5. Bolivia			
6. Chile			
7. Argentina			
8. Paraguay			
9. Uruguay			
10. Brazil			
11. Surinam	X		
12. Guyana	X		
13. French Guiana	X		

14. The countries where Spanish is the official language or one of the official languages are

_____

_____

15. The country where Portuguese is the official language is _____.

16. The country where French is the official language is _____.

17. The country where Dutch is the official language is _____.

18. The country where English is the official language is _____.

© Mark Twain Media, Inc., Publishers

South America   Physical Geography

Name _____ Date _____

Physical Geography

Refer to a map of South America in an atlas or other resource book and answer the following questions. In which country is each physical feature located?

1. The Atacama Desert is located in _____.

2. The Patagonia Plateau is located in _____.

3. The Amazon River is located in _____.

4. Lake Titicaca is located on the border between _____ and _____.

5. Lake Maracaibo is located in _____.

6. The Andes Mountains are located in _____, _____,

_____, _____, _____, _____, and

_____.

7. The Central Valley of Chile is located in _____.

8. The Orinoco River is located in _____.

9. The Straits of Magellan are located in _____.

10. Mt. Chimborazo is located in _____.

Refer to Map I on page 70 and complete the following.

11. Label all the countries of South America.

12. With a red crayon or colored pencil, shade in those countries with territory between $23\frac{1}{2}°$S latitude and $23\frac{1}{2}°$N latitude.

13. The South American nations of _____, _____, and _____ lie on the equator.

14. With a green crayon or colored pencil, shade in those countries that lie north of $23\frac{1}{2}°$N latitude.

15. With a blue crayon or colored pencil, shade in those countries that lie south of $23\frac{1}{2}°$S latitude.

PHYSICAL GEOGRAPHY CROSSWORD PUZZLE

Use the clues below to complete the crossword puzzle. You may need to use an atlas and/or review the geography information given about the countries of South America.

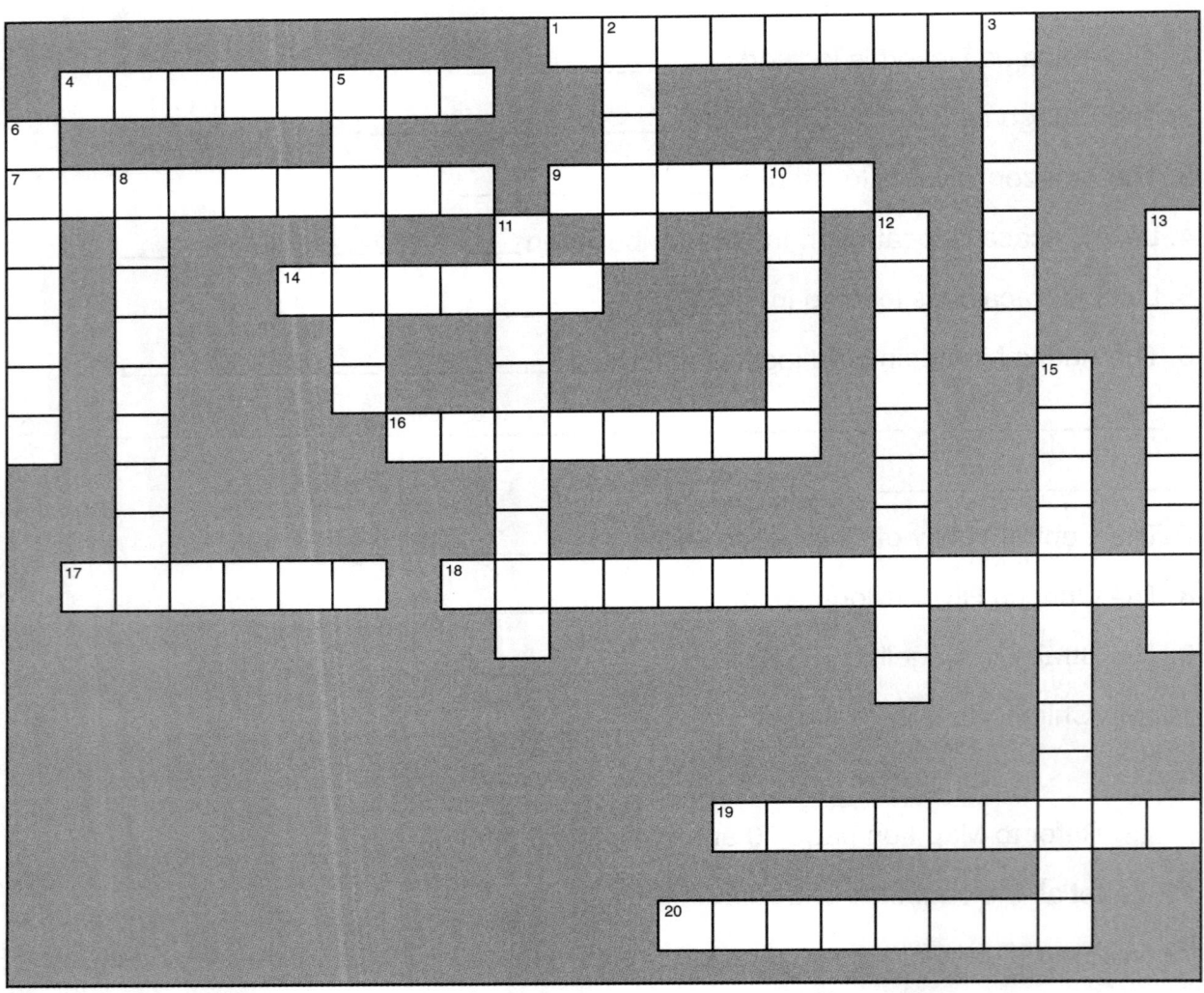

ACROSS
1. Famous lake in Venezuela
4. Volcanic mountain located in Ecuador
7. Subtropical forest areas of Argentina, Paraguay, and Bolivia (two words)
9. Another name for the rain forest region
14. Fertile farming region of Argentina
16. The Straits of _____ are located at the southern tip of South America.
17. River that flows through Brazil, Paraguay, and Argentina
18. Island at the tip of South America (three words)
19. Famous mountain on which there is a statue of Christ that greets visitors to Rio de Janeiro
20. Large lake on the border between Peru and Bolivia

DOWN
2. High mountains extending north to south in South America
3. River in Venezuela
5. Desert in northern Chile
6. Famous waterfall in Brazil
8. Highest mountain in the Americas located in Argentina
10. Famous river near the equator
11. Dry, grassland region of Argentina
12. Highest waterfall in the world located in Venezuela (two words)
13. Pacific islands belonging to Ecuador
15. Large estuary that empties into the Atlantic Ocean (four words)

South America South American Rivers, Lakes, and Mountains Search

Name _____ Date _____

SOUTH AMERICAN RIVERS, LAKES, AND MOUNTAINS SEARCH

Listed below are several of the best-known rivers, lakes, and mountains of South America. On the line beside each item, indicate with an R, L, or M whether it is a river, lake, or mountain, and then find and circle that word in the puzzle. You may need to use an atlas. Words in the puzzle may be printed forward, backward, horizontally, vertically, or diagonally.

```
N A D T X N E W M E Y X N U K M W J H Q
K N O D A L A S L E D S A J O P M V U B
L E G R W I B G E H L S Y A U G A R A P
Q L S L E L E P S G G Y O K F Q K Z X M
T A D V A C A C I T I T S M T W W W J J
O D W L H V H L Z A P J U W T Z H M R W
E G O Q Z A Q I F T Z P A I A O P M M T
F A Y C G P C Y M S D U C P C J E I L J
X M H K M U R R M B X W C W Z R R O Y N
R H T K O C O N I R O X V M A I O V M C
H U A S C A R A N T R R U W M U W F G Y
A V G A H Q E W D C U O A P A M A J A S
I X C N P H V V A S B P C Z Z A C T S Q
S J C A R I P L E I P O J E O N O G K E
Y D A O D V H H A O T P Z B N A N A P V
T U J L L D B C V O E H O U Y R C U M E
N P T A Z R A F P R R M M O N A A L S O
U K R D O R W A L Z W M U D P P G V M B
J W A A A J X Z W N B S B M F O U F N J
Y Q F M A I F N R X U B L C Z V A J R D
```

1. ACONCAGUA ___
2. AMAZON ___
3. CHIMBORAZO ___
4. COTOPAXI ___
5. HUASCARÁN ___
6. MAGDALENA ___
7. MARACAIBO ___
8. MIRIM ___
9. OJAS DEL SALADO ___
10. ORINOCO ___
11. PARAGUAY ___
12. PARANÁ ___
13. POOPÓ ___
14. SAJAMA ___
15. TITICACA ___

© Mark Twain Media, Inc., Publishers

Name _____ Date _____

SOUTH AMERICAN CAPITAL MATCHING

Match the capital city in Column B with the correct country in Column A by placing the letter of the capital on the line next to the corresponding country.

Column A **Column B**

_____ 1. Argentina   A. Asunción
_____ 2. Bolivia   B. Bogotá
_____ 3. Brazil   C. Brasília
_____ 4. Chile   D. Buenos Aires
_____ 5. Colombia   E. Caracas
_____ 6. Ecuador   F. Cayenne
_____ 7. French Guiana   G. Georgetown
_____ 8. Guyana   H. La Paz
_____ 9. Paraguay   I. Lima
_____ 10. Peru   J. Montevideo
_____ 11. Surinam   K. Paramaribo
_____ 12. Uruguay   L. Quito
_____ 13. Venezuela   M. Santiago

CAPITAL MAP EXERCISE

Refer to Map I on page 70. Locate and label the capital cities on the map of South America.

South American Capital Search

The countries of South America are listed below. On the blank beside each one write in that country's capital city. Then, find and circle that capital in the puzzle. Words in the puzzle may be printed forward, backward, horizontally, vertically, or diagonally.

```
N D F U Z K T K A P C K R S B W I I N L
F K O W F D C A R A C A S D D F A L E R
E A A Q X M I L K N G K P O V Y J I U B
F D R Z Z B O G O T A O W N J H U M O R
P M O N T E V I D E O Y J F D T E A P A
K N X O J N V Q J Q Z O W H S N B M T S
T W Z V X O E N Z P G P I R N D D U I I
Z O Q C J I S L B A L D Y E A E D J M L
O T U A G U A N I U Q G Y K A L G X X I
I E D O T N V T C V E A F N K A L C Q A
S G Q M O U N R P Q C N A U D P X H U E
L R L U B A X V A V D F O S E A E M I L
W O B W S T B X E Y G O N S U Z J Y T U
U E F T J Y W Z G L U O X R A N G F O H
C G S O F T D X X K X K L E F I C U U B
V M E N N R O N V A U L B C X S R I N P
V B Y A Z E A Z L G V E L X A S R E O W
A T J P A R A M A R I B O V G U R Y S N
W F S I L G F T C Q S K E B W L L H B Y
Q G I X Q G Y J D H Y B Q O X M Z V Q L
```

1. Colombia: _____
2. Venezuela: _____
3. Ecuador: _____
4. Peru: _____
5. Guyana: _____
6. Surinam: _____
7. French Guiana: _____
8. Brazil: _____
9. Chile: _____
10. Bolivia: _____
11. Argentina: _____
12. Paraguay: _____
13. Uruguay: _____

South America   Demographics: Ranking World Cities by Population

Name _____ Date _____

Demographics

RANKING WORLD CITIES BY POPULATION

The following are the ten largest cities in the world. List the cities in order from largest to smallest on the blanks below. On the blank next to each city, write the name of the country where the city is located. Write the population on the line in the population column for each city.

Calcutta (11,898,000)
São Paulo (18,701,000)
Tokyo/Yokohama (27,245,000)
Buenos Aires (11,657,000)
Bombay (12,101,000)
Mexico City (20,899,000)
Osaka/Kobe/Kyoto (13,872,000)
Seoul (16,792,000)
New York (14,625,000)
Rio de Janeiro (11,688,000)

City	Country	Population
1.		
2.		
3.		
4.		
5.		
6.		
7.		
8.		
9.		
10.		

11. Which cities from the above list are located in South America? _____

_____

12. What is the largest city in South America? _____

13. In what country is the largest city in South America located? _____

South America South American Cities Map Exercise

Name _____ Date _____

SOUTH AMERICAN CITIES MAP EXERCISE

The cities listed below are all large South American cities. Locate the cities on Map I on page 70. Place a dot to locate the city and write the name of the city by the dot.

Recife	**Buenos Aires**	**Caracas**
Guayaquil	**Rio de Janeiro**	**São Paulo**
Montevideo	**Santiago**	**Quito**
Belém	**Barranquilla**	**Lima**
Bogotá	**Medellín**	

Refer to Map I and answer the following questions.

1. The cities located along the coast are: _____
_____
_____

2. Cities located in the Andes Mountains are: _____
_____

Mark each of the following as true (T) or false (F). If you answer false, correct the statement on the blank to make it true.

_____ 3. Many of the large cities of South America are located near the coast.
_____

_____ 4. Chile has more large cities than any other South American nation.
_____

_____ 5. Rio de Janeiro is located in the interior of Brazil.
_____

_____ 6. Most of the people of South America live in cities in the high Andes or in cities near the coast.
_____

_____ 7. The country with the greatest number of large cities is Brazil.
_____

South America | Ranking South American Countries by Area

Name _____ Date _____

RANKING SOUTH AMERICAN COUNTRIES BY AREA

The countries of South America are listed below, along with their areas in square miles. Arrange the countries in the following chart from largest to smallest.

Argentina (1,068,000 sq. mi.)
Brazil (3,286,472 sq. mi.)
Colombia (439,733 sq. mi.)
French Guiana (34,749 sq. mi)
Paraguay (157,046 sq. mi.)
Surinam (63,039 sq. mi.)
Venezuela (352,143 sq. mi.)

Bolivia (424,162 sq. mi.)
Chile (292,258 sq. mi.)
Ecuador (109,483 sq. mi.)
Guyana (83,000 sq. mi.)
Peru (496,223 sq. mi.)
Uruguay (68,498 sq. mi.)

	Country	Area
1.		
2.		
3.		
4.		
5.		
6.		
7.		
8.		
9.		
10.		
11.		
12.		
13.		

14. The area of the United States in square miles is 3,618,765 square miles. Which South American countries are larger than the United States in area?

_____

© Mark Twain Media, Inc., Publishers

South America

Name _____ Date _____

RANKING SOUTH AMERICAN COUNTRIES BY POPULATION

The countries of South America are listed below, along with their populations. Arrange the countries in the following chart from largest to smallest. Place their rank in area, determined in the activity on page 68, in the appropriate column below.

Argentina (34,663,000)
Brazil (161,416,000)
Colombia (34,948,000)
French Guiana (154,000)
Paraguay (4,979,000)
Surinam (421,000)
Venezuela (21,810,000)

Bolivia (7,900,000)
Chile (14,271,000)
Ecuador (11,384,000)
Guyana (832,000)
Peru (23,588,000)
Uruguay (3,186,000)

	Country	Population	Rank in Area
1.			
2.			
3.			
4.			
5.			
6.			
7.			
8.			
9.			
10.			
11.			
12.			
13.			

14. The population of the United States is 263,563,000. Which South American countries are larger than the United States in population?

_____

South America

Map I
South America

South America Map II: Climate Regions of South America

Map II
Climate Regions of South America

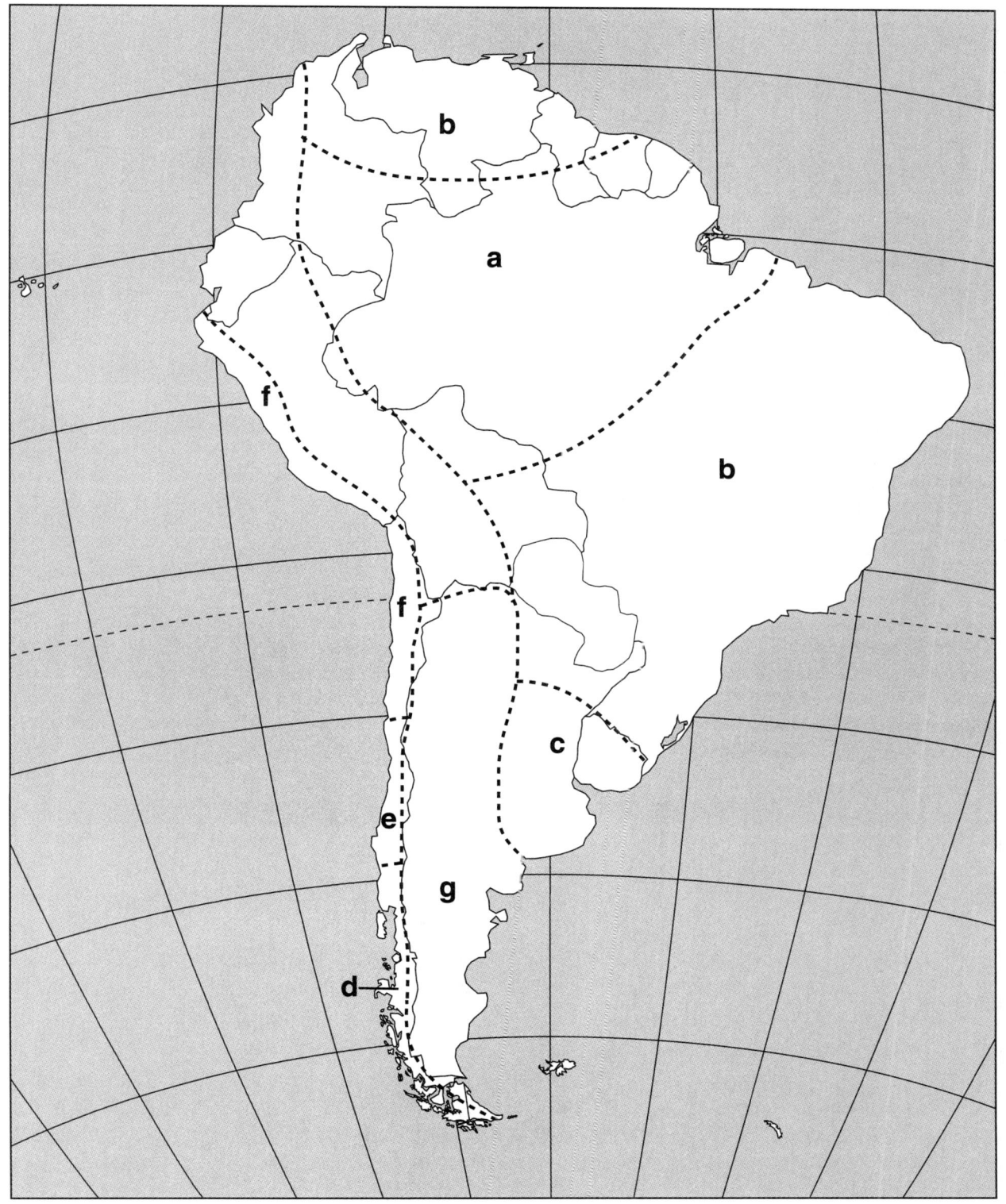

© Mark Twain Media, Inc., Publishers

South America   Map III: Ocean and Wind Currents

Map III
Ocean and Wind Currents

© Mark Twain Media, Inc., Publishers

Map IV
Viceroyalties of South America

Map V
Southern South America: Argentina and Chile

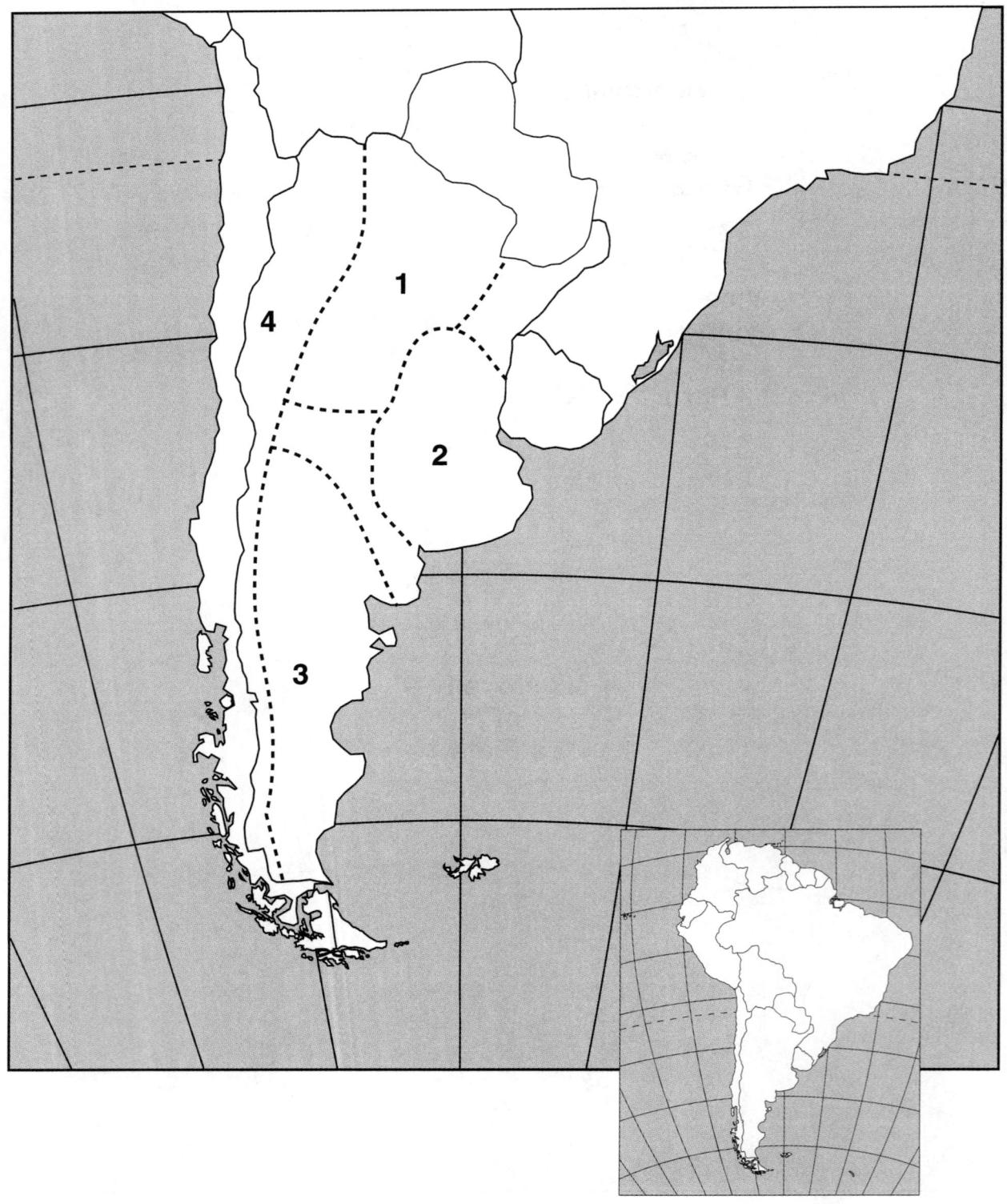

South America   Map VI: Brazil

Map VI
Brazil

Map VII
Northern South America: Colombia, Venezuela, Guyana, Surinam, and French Guiana

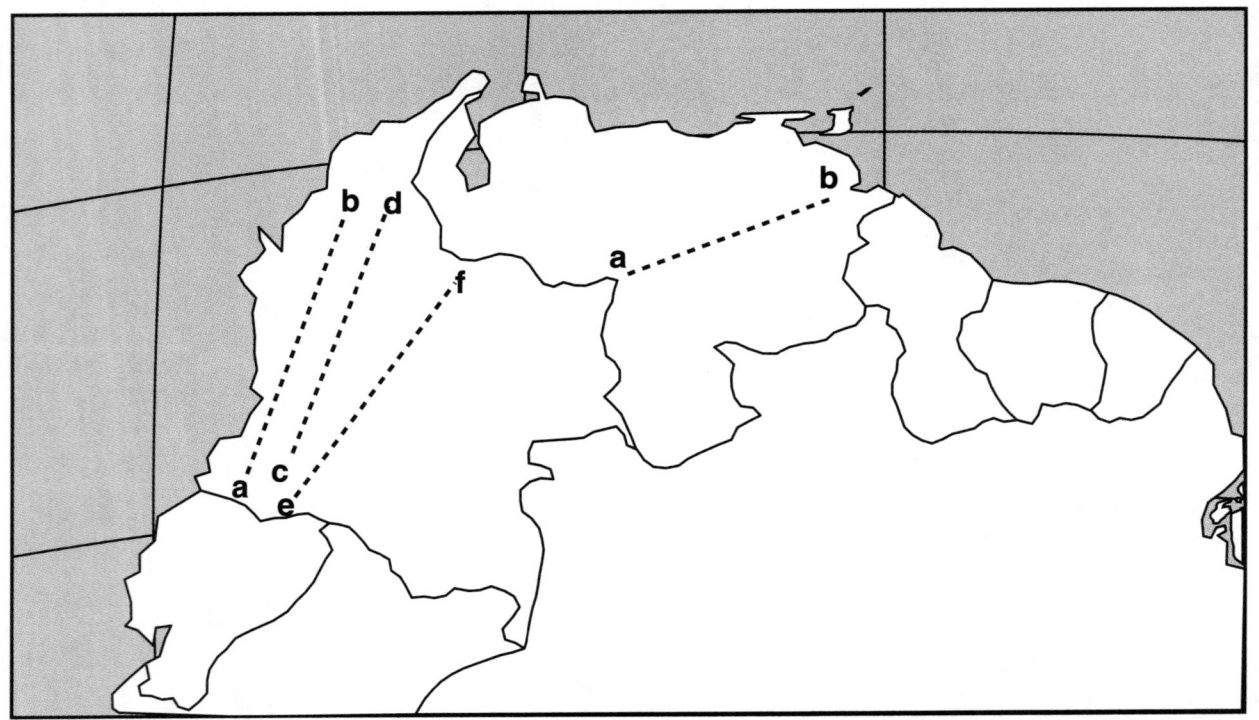

South America   Map VIII: Ecuador, Peru, and Bolivia

Map VIII
Ecuador, Peru, and Bolivia

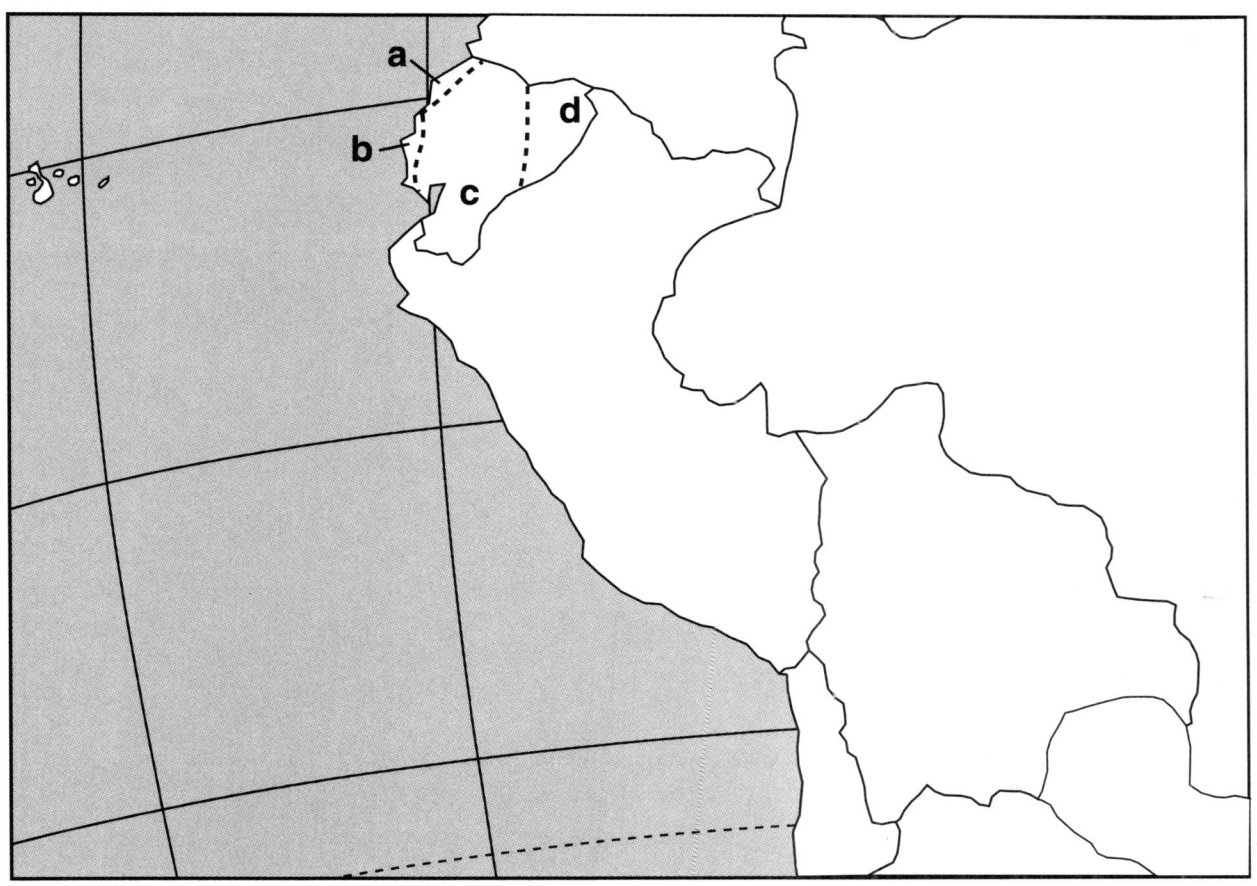

© Mark Twain Media, Inc., Publishers   77

South America

Map IX
Paraguay and Uruguay

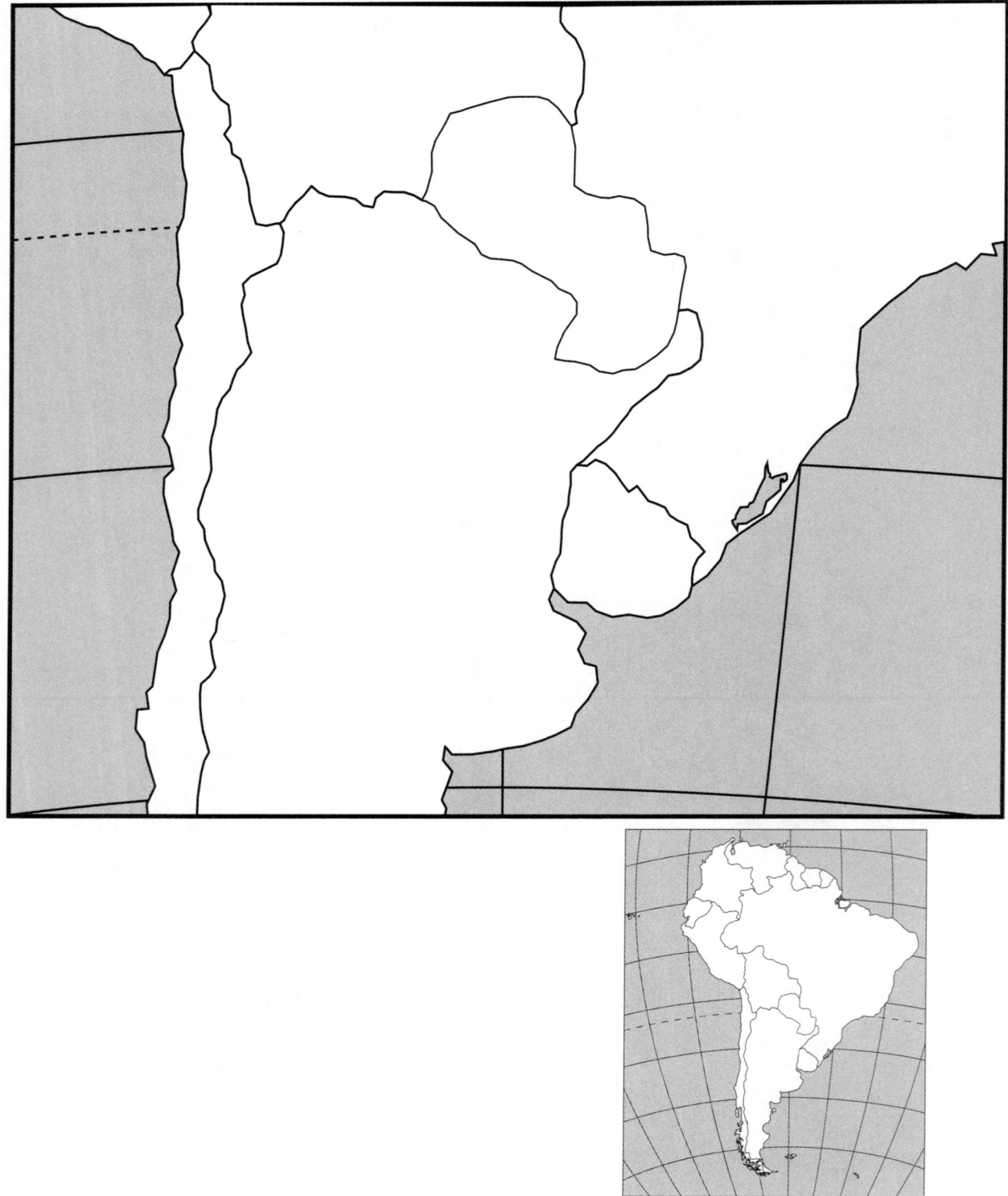

Answer Keys

Learning About Climates in South America (page 1)
4. Ecuador, Colombia, Venezuela, Guyana, Surinam, French Guiana, Brazil
5. Venezuela, Guyana, Surinam, French Guiana
6. Peru, Bolivia, Paraguay, Chile, Argentina, Uruguay
7. Ecuador, Colombia, Brazil

Learning About the Tropics (page 3)
4. Colombia, Venezuela, Guyana, Surinam, French Guiana, Ecuador, Peru, Bolivia
5. Brazil, Paraguay, Chile, Argentina
6. All those countries listed above

Learning About the Seasons (pages 4–5)
1. Northern
2. Southern
3. Southern
4. Northern
5. March, September

6. June
7. December
8. December
9. toward
10. away
11. June
12. December

13. June, July, August, September
14. December, January, February, March
15. December, January, February, March
16. June, July, August, September
17. summer
18. winter
19. tilt
20. revolution

Daylight and Darkness in the Tropics (page 6)
1. 12 hours, 7 minutes
2. 10 hours, 56 minutes; 13 hours, 20 minutes
3. 8 hours, 5 minutes; 16 hours, 21 minutes
4. 0 hours, 0 minutes; 24 hours, 0 minutes
5. Since the higher latitudes are farther from the equator, the tilt of the earth has a much greater effect on those latitudes.

South America   Answer Keys

Temperature in the Tropics (pages 7–9)
1. 80
2. 65
3. 53
4. The higher the altitude, the lower the temperature.
8. Teacher check graph
9. Manaus is close to sea level, but Quito is at a high altitude, so it is cooler and drier.

10.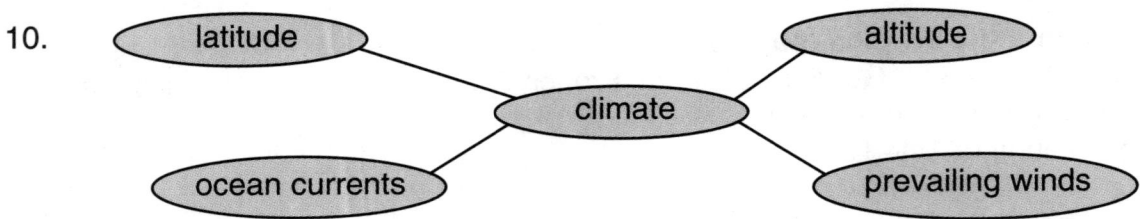

11. Tierra del Fuego
12. ~53–56
13. Southern

Climates in South America (page 11)
8. Brazil; Bolivia; Peru; East Coast; Equator; Hot, Wet
9. Brazil; Argentina; Bolivia; East Coast; Hot, Wet; Dry
10. Argentina; East Coast; Hot, Wet
11. Chile; West Coast
12. Chile; West Coast; Dry
13. Chile; Peru; West Coast; Dry
14. Argentina; East Coast; Dry

The Effects of Currents and Winds on Climate (page 12)
1. (a) warm, (b) equator
2. (a) cold, (b) pole

Learning About El Niño: Reviewing What I Have Learned (page 15)
1. Peruvian Current
2. fog
3. cool current
4. plankton
5. fishermen
6. warm current
7. El Niño
8. rainfall
9. flooding
10. weather

11–20. Teacher check

Incas: Reviewing What I Have Learned (page 21)
1. conquistadors
2. Inca
3. Great Ruler
4. Cuzco
5. Machu Picchu
6. Quechan
7. terraces
8. Ecuador
9. Bolivia
10. Chile
11. roads
12. chasquis
13. Sun
14. calendar
15. craftsmen
16. gold
17. gold
18. conquistadors
19. quipu
20. colors

Indians of the Amazon: Reviewing What I Have Learned (page 24)
1. hunting
2. fishing
3. slash-and-burn
4. infertile
5. manioc
6. yam
7. advanced
8. Inca
9. modern
10. plantations

Araucanian Indians: Reviewing What I Have Learned (page 24)
1. conquistador
2. Chile
3. Araucanians
4. warrior
5. Andes
6. Argentina
7. plains
8. North America
9. reservations
10. cultural

South America   Answer Keys

Spanish Rule Map Exercise (page 25)
2. four
3. Viceroyalty of New Granada, Viceroyalty of Peru, Viceroyalty of La Plata

Spanish Rule and Independence Crossword Puzzle (page 27)

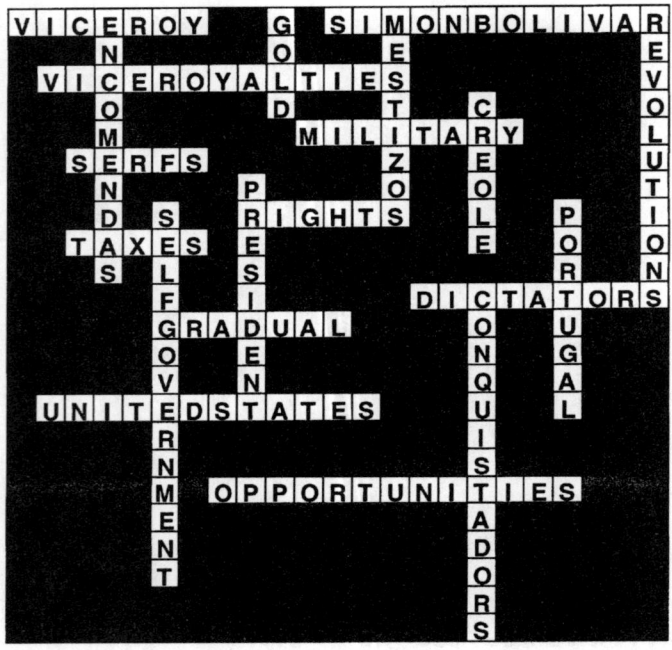

Animals of South America: Reviewing What I Have Learned (page 29)
1. monkeys
2. Dinosaur
3. Patagonia
4. Argentina
5. alpaca
6. vicuña
7. guanaco
8. llama
9. alpaca
10. vicuña
11. llama
12. wool
13. armadillo
14. ball
15. tapir
16. water
17. land
18. sloth
19. claw
20. trees

Argentina: Reviewing What I Have Learned (page 34)
Physical Features of Argentina

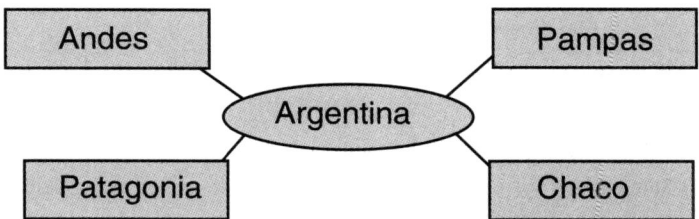

Matching
1. J
2. G
3. A
4. H
5. B
6. C
7. I
8. E
9. F
10. D

Brazil: Reviewing What I Have Learned (page 37)
1. Brasília
2. São Paulo
3. Belém
4. Rio de Janeiro
5. Recife
6. Belo Horizonte

Crops/Livestock
sugar
corn
soybeans
cattle
coffee

Natural Resources
iron ore
petroleum

Venezuela: Reviewing What I Have Learned (page 39)
1. G   6. H
2. D   7. I
3. F   8. B
4. A   9. J
5. C   10. E

Colombia: Reviewing What I Have Learned (page 41)

Colombia

Highland Cities	Port Cities	Natural Resources	Crops
Bogotá	Cartagena	emeralds	bananas
Medellín	Barranquilla	gold	sugar cane
Cali		coal	coffee
		oil	cotton
		iron ore	

Ecuador (page 43)

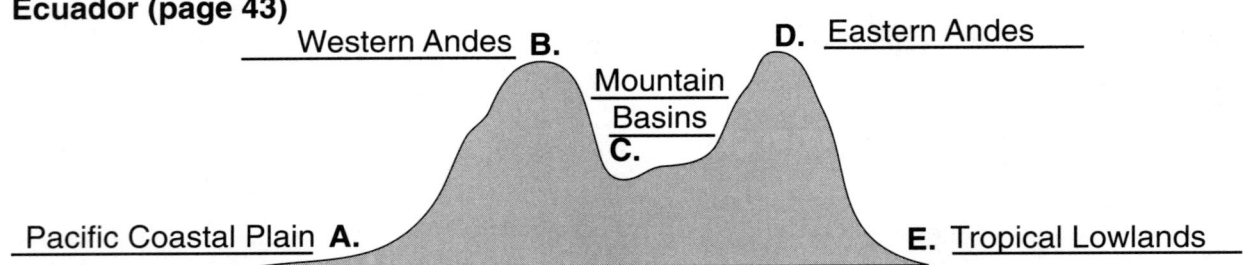

A. Pacific Coastal Plain
B. Western Andes
C. Mountain Basins
D. Eastern Andes
E. Tropical Lowlands

Peru (page 45)
Matching
1. D
2. E
3. B
4. F
5. C
6. A
7. G

Pacific Coastal Area
commercial farming
cotton
sugar cane
rice
dry
hot

High Plateaus
subsistance farming
corn
beans
potatoes
grains
cool

Eastern Tropical Area
oil production
oil
hot
wet

Bolivia (page 47)
1. Altiplano
2. subsistence
3. rye
4. potatoes
5. beans
6. Titicaca

Bolivia (continued)
7. warmer
8. tin
9. silver
10. oil
11. La Paz
12. Sucre
13. Indians
14. Mestizos
15. European

Peru, Ecuador, and Bolivia: Reviewing What I Have Learned (page 48)
1. Mt. Chimborazo
2. Mt. Cotopaxi
3. Quito
4. Guayaquil
5. Ecuador
6. Peru
7. Colombia
8. La Paz
9. Bolivia
10. Sucre
11. Chile
12. Argentina
13. Paraguay
14. Brazil
15. Peru
16. Callao
17. Lima
18. Cuzco
19. Amazon River
20. Iquitos

Chile (page 50)

Northern Chile	Central Chile	Southern Chile
Atacama Desert	mild, moist winters	chilly, wet winters
copper	grapes	cool summers
very dry	fruits	glaciers
Antofagasta	wheat	
	cattle	
	agricultural area	
	warm summers	
	Valparaíso	
	Santiago	
	Concepción	

Chile: Reviewing What I Have Learned (page 51)
1. Peru
2. Bolivia
3. Cape Horn
4. 2,600
5. 260
6. Central Valley
7. Atacama
8. El Niño
9. Mestizo
10. Italy

Ecuador	**Peru**	**Bolivia**	**Chile**
Andes	Andes	Andes	Andes
Spanish	Spanish	Spanish	Spanish
Equator	Altiplano	Altiplano	desert
oil	oil	oil	copper
desert	desert	landlocked	Mestizo
Mestizo/Indian	Indian	Mestizo	

Paraguay (page 53)
1. December, January, February
2. June, July, August
3. December, January, February, March
4. June, July, August, September
5. (a) in the tropics
6. October, November, December, January
7. June, July, August

Paraguay: Reviewing What I Have Learned (page 54)
1. (a) Spanish, (b) Guaraní
2. Mestizos
3. Paraná, Paraguay
4. Yerba Mate
5. landlocked
6. quebracho
7. subsistence
8. Brazil
9. hydroelectric
10. Guaraní

Paraguay Crossword Puzzle (page 55)

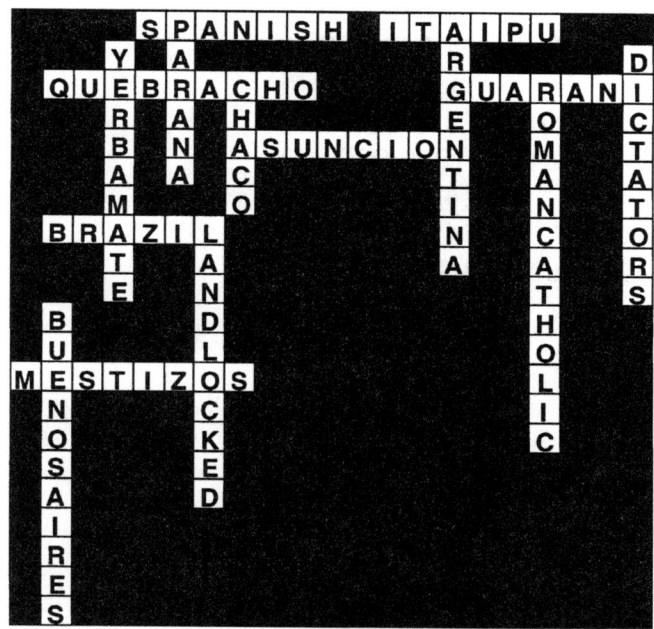

Uruguay: Reviewing What I Have Learned (page 57)
1. seventeenth
2. Portuguese
3. Montevideo
4. Viceroyalty
5. Brazil
6. Argentina
7. water
8. estuary
9. Rio Negro
10. rainy

Agricultural	**Industry**
beef	textiles
wool	leather goods
hides	cement
trees	tires
maize	food processing and packing
potatoes	hydroelectric power
sugar beets	light engineering
wheat	steel
	tourism

South American Countries: Reviewing What I Have Learned (page 60)

1. Venezuela	Catholic	Spanish	21,810,000
2. Colombia	Catholic	Spanish	34,948,000
3. Ecuador	Catholic	Spanish	11,384,000
4. Peru	Catholic	Spanish/Quechua	23,588,000
5. Bolivia	Catholic	Sp./Que./Aymara	7,900,000
6. Chile	Catholic	Spanish	14,271,000
7. Argentina	Catholic	Spanish	34,663,000
8. Paraguay	Catholic	Spanish/Guaraní	4,979,000
9. Uruguay	Catholic	Spanish	3,186,000
10. Brazil	Catholic	Portuguese	161,416,000
11. Surinam	X	Dutch	421,000
12. Guyana	X	English	832,000
13. French Guiana	X	French	154,000

Physical Geography (page 61)
1. Chile
2. Argentina
3. Brazil
4. Peru, Bolivia
5. Venezuela
6. Venezuela, Colombia, Ecuador, Peru, Bolivia, Chile, Argentina
7. Chile
8. Venezuela
9. Chile
10. Ecuador

13. Ecuador, Colombia, Brazil

Physical Geography Crossword Puzzle (page 62)

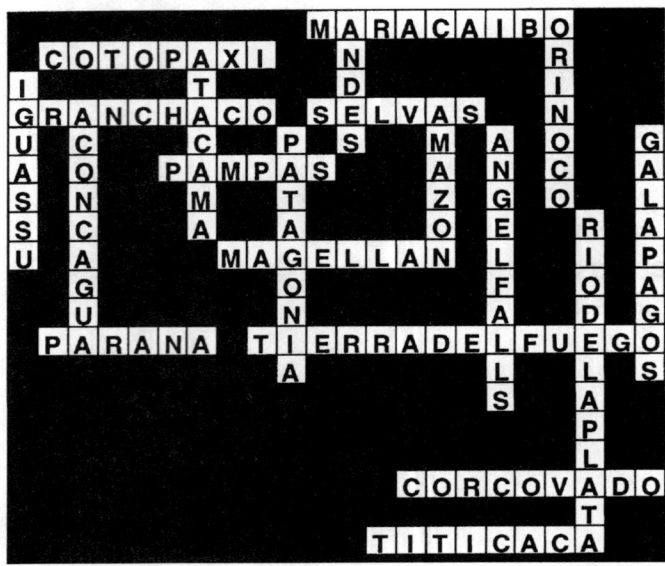

South American Rivers, Lakes, and Mountains Search (page 63)

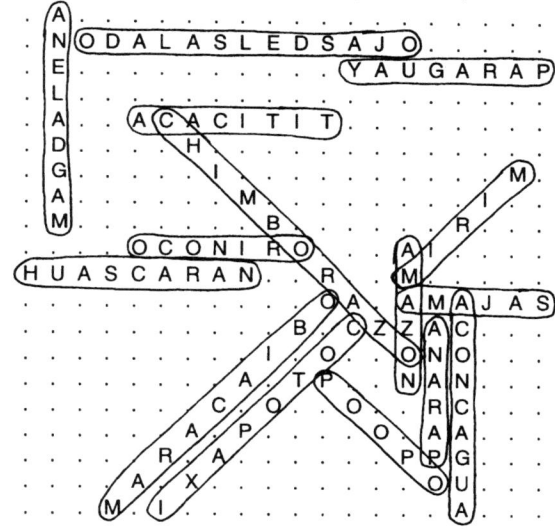

1. M
2. R
3. M
4. M
5. M
6. R
7. L
8. L
9. M
10. R
11. R
12. R
13. L
14. M
15. L

South American Capital Matching (page 64)

1. D
2. H
3. C
4. M
5. B
6. L
7. F
8. G
9. A
10. I
11. K
12. J
13. E

South American Capital Search (page 65)

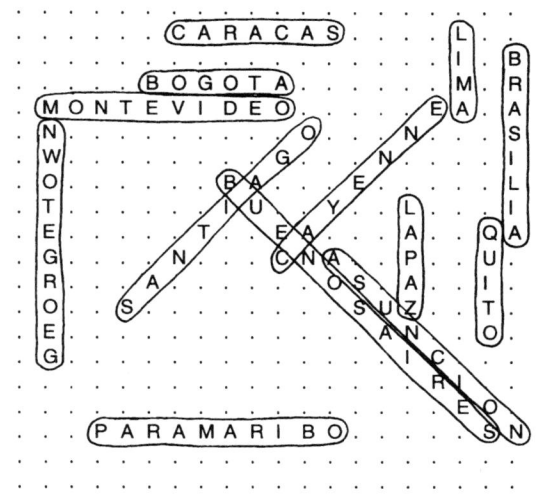

1. Bogotá
2. Caracas
3. Quito
4. Lima
5. Georgetown
6. Paramaribo
7. Cayenne
8. Brasília
9. Santiago
10. La Paz
11. Buenos Aires
12. Asunción
13. Montevideo

Ranking World Cities by Population (page 66)
1. Tokyo/Yokohama; Japan; 27,345,000
2. Mexico City; Mexico; 20,899,000
3. São Paulo; Brazil; 18,701,000
4. Seole; South Korea; 16,792,000
5. New York; United States; 14,625,000
6. Osaka/Kobe/Kyoto; Japan; 13,872,000
7. Bombay; India; 12,101,000
8. Calcutta; India; 11,898,000
9. Rio de Janeira; Brazil; 11,688,000
10. Buenos Aires; Argentina; 11,657,000
11. São Paulo, Buenos Aires, Rio de Janeiro
12. São Paulo
13. Brazil

South American Cities Map Exercise (page 67)
1. Recife, Guayaquil, Montevideo, Belém, Buenos Aires, Rio de Janeiro, São Paulo, Lima, Barranquilla
2. Santiago, Medellín, Bogotá, Caracas, Quito
3. T
4. F; Brazil has more large cities than any other South American nation.
5. F; Rio de Janeiro is located on the coast of Brazil.
6. T
7. T

Ranking South American Countries by Area (page 68)
1. Brazil; 3,286,472 sq. mi.
2. Argentina; 1,068,000 sq. mi.
3. Peru; 496,223 sq. mi.
4. Colombia; 439,733 sq. mi.
5. Bolivia; 424,162 sq. mi.
6. Venezuela; 352,143 sq. mi.
7. Chile; 292,258 sq. mi.
8. Paraguay; 157,046 sq. mi.
9. Ecuador; 109,483 sq. mi.
10. Guyana; 83,000 sq. mi.
11. Uruguay; 68,498 sq. mi.
12. Surinam; 63,039 sq. mi.
13. French Guiana; 34,749 sq. mi.

14. None

Ranking South American Countries by Population (page 69)
1. Brazil; 161,416,000; 1
2. Colombia; 34,948,000; 4
3. Argentina; 34,663,000; 2
4. Peru; 23,588,000; 3
5. Venezuela; 21,810,000; 6
6. Chile; 14,271,000; 7
7. Ecuador; 11,384,000; 9
8. Bolivia; 7,900,000; 5
9. Paraguay; 4,979,000; 8
10. Uruguay; 3,186,000; 11
11. Guyana; 832,000; 10
12. Surinam; 421,000; 12
13. French Guiana; 154,000; 13

14. None

Bibliography

Bacon, Phillip. *World Geography, The Earth and Its People.* Dallas: Harcourt Brace Jovanovich, 1989.

Boehm, Richard G. *World Geography, A Physical and Cultural Approach.* New York: Macmillian/McGraw Hill, 1995.

Crystal, David (editor). *The Cambridge Factfinder.* Cambridge: Cambridge University Press, 1993.

Lye, Keith. *The Portable World Factbook.* New York: Avon Books, 1997.

Quick Reference World Atlas. Chicago: Rand McNally & Company, 1995.

Willett, B. M. and Gaylord, David (editors). *The Portable World Pocket Atlas.* New York: Avon Books, 1997.